Gloria Estefan

Consulting Editors

Rodolfo Cardona
professor of Spanish
and comparative literature,
Boston University

James Cockcroft
visiting professor of Latin American
and Caribbean studies,
State University of New York at Albany

Hispanics of Achievement

Gloria Estefan

Rebecca Stefoff

Chelsea House Publishers
New York   Philadelphia

CHELSEA HOUSE PUBLISHERS

Editor-in-Chief: Remmel Nunn
Managing Editor: Karyn Gullen Browne
Copy Chief: Juliann Barbato
Picture Editor: Adrian G. Allen
Art Director: Maria Epes
Deputy Copy Chief: Mark Rifkin
Assistant Art Director: Noreen Romano
Manufacturing Manager: Gerald Levine
Systems Manager: Lindsey Ottman
Production Manager: Joseph Romano
Production Coordinator: Marie Claire Cebrián

Hispanics of Achievement
Senior Editor: John W. Selfridge

Staff for GLORIA ESTEFAN
Associate Editor: Philip Koslow
Copy Editor: Joseph Roman
Editorial Assistant: Martin Mooney
Picture Researcher: Joan Beard
Cover Illustration: Rodrigo Sanz

5 7 9 8 6 4

Library of Congress Cataloging-in-Publication Data
Stefoff, Rebecca
  Gloria Estefan/Rebecca Stefoff
     p. cm.—(Hispanics of achievement)
  Includes bibliographical references and index.
  Summary: Profiles the Cuban-American pop singer who is the
leader of the popular Latin musical group the Miami Sound
Machine
  ISBN 0-7910-1244-1
        0-7910-1635-8 (pbk.)
   1. Estefan, Gloria—Juvenile literature. 2. Singers—United States—
Biography—Juvenile literature. [Estefan, Gloria. 2. Singers 3.
Cuban Americans—Biography. 4. Rock music.]
I. Title II. Series
ML3930.E85S7 1991
782.42164'092—dc20   90-26286
[B]   CIP
[92]   MN AC

Contents

Hispanics of Achievement

Oscar Arias Sánchez
Costa Rican president

Joan Baez
Mexican-American folksinger

Rubén Blades
Panamanian lawyer and entertainer

Jorge Luis Borges
Argentine writer

Juan Carlos
king of Spain

Pablo Casals
Spanish cellist and conductor

Miguel de Cervantes
Spanish writer

Cesar Chavez
Mexican-American labor leader

El Cid
Spanish military leader

Roberto Clemente
Puerto Rican baseball player

Plácido Domingo
Spanish singer

El Greco
Spanish artist

Gloria Estefan
Cuban-American singer

Gabriel García Márquez
Colombian writer

Raul Julia
Puerto Rican actor

Diego Maradona
Argentine soccer player

José Martí
Cuban revolutionary and poet

Rita Moreno
Puerto Rican singer and actress

Pablo Neruda
Chilean poet and diplomat

Antonia Novello
U.S. surgeon general

Octavio Paz
Mexican poet and critic

Javier Pérez de Cuéllar
Peruvian diplomat

Anthony Quinn
Mexican-American actor

Diego Rivera
Mexican artist

Antonio López de Santa Anna
Mexican general and politician

George Santayana
Spanish poet and philosopher

Junípero Serra
Spanish missionary and explorer

Lee Trevino
Mexican-American golfer

Pancho Villa
Mexican revolutionary

CHELSEA HOUSE PUBLISHERS

INTRODUCTION

Hispanics of Achievement

Rodolfo Cardona

The Spanish language and many other elements of Spanish culture are present in the United States today and have been since the country's earliest beginnings. Some of these elements have come directly from the Iberian Peninsula; others have come indirectly, by way of Mexico, the Caribbean basin, and the countries of Central and South America.

Spanish culture has influenced America in many subtle ways, and consequently many Americans remain relatively unaware of the extent of its impact. The vast majority of them recognize the influence of Spanish culture in America, but they often do not realize the great importance and long history of that influence. This is partly because Americans have tended to judge the Hispanic influence in the United States in statistical terms rather than to look closely at the ways in which individual Hispanics have profoundly affected American culture. For this reason, it is fitting that Americans obtain more than a passing acquaintance with the origins of these Spanish cultural elements and gain an understanding of how they have been woven into the fabric of American society.

It is well documented that Spanish seafarers were the first to explore and colonize many of the early territories of what is today called the United States of America. For this reason, students of geography discover Hispanic names all over the map of the United States. For instance, the Strait of Juan de Fuca was named after the Spanish explorer who first navigated the waters of the Pacific Northwest; the names of states such as Arizona (arid zone), Montana (mountain), Florida (thus named because it was reached on Easter Sunday, which in Spanish is called the feast of Pascua Florida), and California (named after a fictitious land in one of the first and probably the most popular among the Spanish novels of chivalry, *Amadis of Gaul*) are all derived from Spanish; and there are numerous mountains, rivers, canyons, towns, and cities with Spanish names throughout the United States.

Not only explorers but many other illustrious figures in Spanish history have helped define American culture. For example, the 13th-century king of Spain, Alfonso X, also known as the Learned, may be unknown to the majority of Americans, but his work on the codification of Spanish law has greatly influenced the evolution of American law, particularly in the jurisdictions of the Southwest. For this contribution a statue of him stands in the rotunda of the Capitol in Washington, D.C. Likewise, the name Diego Rivera may be unfamiliar to most Americans, but this Mexican painter influenced many American artists whose paintings, commissioned during the Great Depression and the New Deal era of the 1930s, adorn the walls of government buildings throughout the United States. In recent years the contributions of Puerto Ricans, Mexicans, Mexican Americans (Chicanos), and Cubans in American cities such as Boston, Chicago, Los Angeles,

Miami, Minneapolis, New York, and San Antonio have been enormous.

The importance of the Spanish language in this vast cultural complex cannot be overstated. Spanish, after all, is second only to English as the most widely spoken of Western languages within the United States as well as in the entire world. The popularity of the Spanish language in America has a long history.

In addition to Spanish exploration of the New World, the great Spanish literary tradition served as a vehicle for bringing the language and culture to America. Interest in Spanish literature in America began when English immigrants brought with them translations of Spanish masterpieces of the Golden Age. As early as 1683, private libraries in Philadelphia and Boston contained copies of the first picaresque novel, *Lazarillo de Tormes*, translations of Francisco de Quevedo's *Los Sueños*, and copies of the immortal epic of reality and illusion *Don Quixote*, by the great Spanish writer Miguel de Cervantes. It would not be surprising if Cotton Mather, the arch-Puritan, read *Don Quixote* in its original Spanish, if only to enrich his vocabulary in preparation for his writing *La fe del cristiano en 24 artículos de la Institución de Cristo, enviada a los españoles para que abran sus ojos* (The Christian's Faith in 24 Articles of the Institution of Christ, Sent to the Spaniards to Open Their Eyes), published in Boston in 1699.

Over the years, Spanish authors and their works have had a vast influence on American literature—from Washington Irving, John Steinbeck, and Ernest Hemingway in the novel to Henry Wadsworth Longfellow and Archibald MacLeish in poetry. Such important American writers as James Fenimore Cooper, Edgar Allan Poe, Walt Whitman, Mark Twain, and Herman Melville all owe a sizable debt to the Spanish literary tradition. Some writers, such as Willa Cather and Maxwell Anderson, who explored Spanish themes they came into contact with in the American Southwest and Mexico, were influenced less directly but no less profoundly.

Important contributions to a knowledge of Spanish culture in the United States were also made by many lesser known individuals—teachers, publishers, historians, entrepreneurs, and others—with a love for Spanish culture. One of the most significant of these contributions was made by Abiel Smith, a Harvard College graduate of the class of 1764, when he bequeathed stock worth $20,000 to Harvard for the support of a professor of French and Spanish. By 1819 this endowment had produced enough income to appoint a professor, and the philologist and humanist George Ticknor became the first holder of the Abiel Smith Chair, which was the very first endowed Chair at Harvard University. Other illustrious holders of the Smith Chair would include the poets Henry Wadsworth Longfellow and James Russell Lowell.

A highly respected teacher and scholar, Ticknor was also a collector of Spanish books, and as such he made a very special contribution to America's knowledge of Spanish culture. He was instrumental in amassing for Harvard libraries one of the first and most impressive collections of Spanish books in the United States. He also had a valuable personal collection of Spanish books and manuscripts, which he bequeathed to the Boston Public Library.

With the creation of the Abiel Smith Chair, Spanish language and literature courses became part of the curriculum at Harvard, which also went on to become the first American university to offer graduate studies in Romance languages. Other colleges and universities throughout the United States gradually followed Harvard's example, and today Spanish language and culture may be studied at most American institutions of higher learning.

No discussion of the Spanish influence in the United States, however brief, would be complete without a mention of the Spanish influence on art. Important American artists such as John Singer Sargent, James A. M. Whistler, Thomas Eakins, and Mary Cassatt all explored Spanish subjects and experimented with Spanish techniques. Virtually every serious American artist living today has studied the work of the Spanish masters as well as the great 20th-century Spanish painters Salvador Dalí, Joan Miró, and Pablo Picasso.

The most pervasive Spanish influence in America, however, has probably been in music. Compositions such as Leonard Bernstein's *West Side Story*, the Latinization of William Shakespeare's *Romeo and Juliet* set in New York's Puerto Rican quarter, and Aaron Copland's *Salon Mexico* are two obvious examples. In general, one can hear the influence of Latin rhythms—from tango to mambo, from guaracha to salsa—in virtually every form of American music.

This series of biographies, which Chelsea House has published under the general title HISPANICS OF ACHIEVEMENT, constitutes further recognition of—and a renewed effort to bring forth to the consciousness of America's young people—the contributions that Hispanic people have made not only in the United States but throughout the civilized world. The men and women who are featured in this series have attained a high level of accomplishment in their respective fields of endeavor and have made a permanent mark on American society.

The title of this series must be understood in its broadest possible sense: The term *Hispanics* is intended to include Spaniards, Spanish Americans, and individuals from many countries whose language and culture have either direct or indirect Spanish origins. The names of many of the people included in this series will be immediately familiar; others will be less recognizable. All, however, have attained recognition within their own countries, and often their fame has transcended their borders.

The series HISPANICS OF ACHIEVEMENT thus addresses the attainments and struggles of Hispanic people in the United States and seeks to tell the stories of individuals whose personal and professional lives in some way reflect the larger Hispanic experience. These stories are exemplary of what human beings can accomplish, often against daunting odds and by extraordinary personal sacrifice, where there is conviction and determination.

Fray Junípero Serra, the 18th-century Spanish Franciscan missionary, is one such individual. Although in very poor health, he devoted the last 15 years of his life to the foundation of missions throughout California—then a mostly unsettled expanse of land—in an effort to bring a better life to Native Americans through the cultivation of crafts and animal husbandry. An example from recent times, the Mexican-American labor leader Cesar Chavez has battled bitter opposition and made untold personal sacrifices in his effort to help poor agricultural workers who have been exploited for decades on farms throughout the Southwest.

The talent with which each one of these men and women may have been endowed required dedication and hard work to develop and become fully realized. Many of them have enjoyed rewards for their efforts during their own lifetime, whereas others have died poor and unrecognized. For some it took a long time to achieve their goals, for others success came at an early age, and for still others the struggle continues. All of them, however, stand out as people whose lives have made a difference, whose achievements we need to recognize today and should continue to honor in the future.

Gloria Estefan

Gloria Estefan meets with President George Bush in the White House on March 19, 1990. During Estefan's visit, the president praised her for a billboard campaign in which she warned young people about the dangers of drug abuse. The following day, on her way to a concert date, Estefan was involved in a near-fatal accident.

CHAPTER ONE

"My Back Is Broken"

It was snowing in Pennsylvania on March 20, 1990. In the eastern part of the state, near a small town called Tobyhanna, not far from the New York State line, Highway I-380 snakes through the Pocono Mountains, winding past rugged granite outcrops and tree-covered peaks. Gusts of wind scattered flurries of wet snow across the highway that day, and the moisture froze into slick, icy patches on the road's dark surface.

On a typical winter weekend, I-380 is jammed with festive weekenders from Philadelphia and New York City, heading for the Pocono resorts with skis strapped to the roofs of their cars. But this was a Tuesday, and the traffic consisted mostly of semis, big tractor-trailer trucks hauling cargo. Sandwiched between two semis in the westbound lane was a large private bus called the Odyssey.

Half a dozen people were aboard the Odyssey that day. The tour bus had been hired by 32-year-old pop singer Gloria Estefan and her 37-year-old husband and manager, Emilio Estefan, Jr. Their nine-year-old son, Nayib; Nayib's tutor, Lori Rooney; and

Gloria Estefan's assistant, Jelissa Arencibia, were also on the bus. They were on their way to Syracuse, New York, where Gloria Estefan and her band, the Miami Sound Machine (MSM), had been scheduled to perform at a concert.

March had been an exhausting but exciting month for the Estefans. Since the first of the month, MSM had been on the road for the concert tour they called Get on Your Feet, after one of the songs on their most recent album. All of the concert appearances were sold out, and the album—titled *Cuts Both Ways*—was a hit around the world. There was talk of taking the tour to South America after it closed in Ohio at the end of March. Videos from the album were frequently shown on music television stations. Some of these videos showed the slim and stylish Gloria Estefan crooning romantic ballads she had written; others showed her cavorting athletically around the stage while belting out MSM's trademark Latin-inspired dance tunes. Estefan had just finished doing a billboard campaign in which she lent her well-known face to the war on drugs, telling young people, "If you need someone, call a friend. Don't do drugs." Just the day before, the Estefan family had been guests at the White House, where President George Bush congratulated Gloria for her antidrug work.

Fame and recognition had been a long time coming for Gloria Estefan. Hers was a story not of overnight success but rather of challenges overcome. Her parents were political refugees who brought her from Cuba to the United States when she was less than two years old. As a Spanish-speaking child in the American South, she battled the insecurity and pain of feeling like an outsider, and as a teenager she shouldered the burden of helping to care for both her younger sister and her invalid father. After she met Emilio Estefan and joined his band as a singer, the group spent a decade performing and recording in Spanish—first at parties and in small clubs; later in concert halls near their home base in Miami, Florida, and throughout Latin America. Over the years, MSM gained popularity with Latin audiences and became one of the most successful groups in Central and South America. But the group remained virtually unknown in the United States until Emilio Estefan convinced their recording company to let them record a song in English. Only then did Gloria Estefan and MSM break out of the recording industry's "Latin music" category to reach a wider audience. Now, with her fourth English-language album near the top of the charts around the world, Estefan had proved that she could appeal to listeners of all kinds, not just to those who shared her Latin roots—although she remained wildly popular with Cuban Americans and others of Hispanic background. She had achieved star status. On March 20 she had only a little more than a week to go until the end of the Get on Your Feet tour, when she would be able to get off her own feet and relax for a few days.

The night before the bus trip, the Estefans had attended a dinner in New York, where they visited with Spanish pop singer Julio Iglesias, a longtime friend. The following morning, they boarded the bus for the trip to Syracuse. Emilio had suggested flying, but Gloria preferred the bus—she thought it would be more restful. Although she had flown many thousands of miles in the past decade, she always felt safer traveling on the ground. "I loved the bus," she later said. "If you crash, at least you're not falling 37,000 feet."

Soon after the bus left New York City, Estefan decided to take a nap so that she would be well rested for that evening's concert. She stretched out on a built-in couch and popped a videocassette—one that she described as "the worst spy movie we had"—into the bus's VCR, knowing that it would lull her to sleep. She fell asleep an hour later. Nayib was studying with his tutor in the rear of the bus; at the front, Emilio was talking on the telephone, which Gloria called "his home away from home."

About 45 minutes later, she woke up. The sun had been shining brightly in a clear sky when she lay down for her nap, but the weather had changed dramatically while she slept. Now the sky

Rescue workers gather at the site of the accident involving Gloria Estefan, on Highway I-380 in Pennsylvania. Estefan's tour bus, the Odyssey (left), was struck in the rear by a tractor trailer (right). The impact of the crash hurled the bus forward into a second trailer truck.

was a dark gray, and snow was falling. She realized why she had awakened—the bus had come to a stop. Emilio was standing not far from Gloria, in the stairwell of the bus, talking on the phone to María Elena Guerriero, the band's secretary in Miami. He was telling her that the bus had halted because there was an accident blocking the road ahead.

According to the Pennsylvania State Police, a tractor-trailer had jackknifed across the highway, bringing traffic to a standstill. The semi in front of the Estefans' bus stopped, and so did the bus, which sat for about three minutes with its motor idling, waiting for the road to be cleared. Guerriero remembered that Emilio Estefan had been describing the scenery to her: "He was telling me how it was snowing and how beautiful it was. We were talking, and suddenly, I lost him."

Emilio Estefan's telephone conversation was cut off in midsentence at 12:15 P.M. when a semi slammed into the Odyssey from behind. To Gloria, it seemed "like an explosion." The force of the impact threw her from the couch (the bus was not equipped with seat belts). At that moment, she entered a world of excruciating pain. She felt a strange tingling in her mouth, something she described as an "electrical" or "metallic" taste, and knew instantly that something was seriously wrong. She cried out, "What happened?" Before Emilio could answer her, the bus was jolted by another crash. The first impact had hurled the Odyssey forward, and now its front end slammed into the parked semi that had been ahead of it on the road. Gloria later discovered that the first jolt, the one that threw her to the floor, had also knocked Emilio right out of his shoes. In the instant between the first and second impacts, she looked up and saw the bus driver, Ron "Bear" Jones, lean sideways to help Emilio. That movement probably saved Jones's life, for when the bus crashed into the semi in front of it,

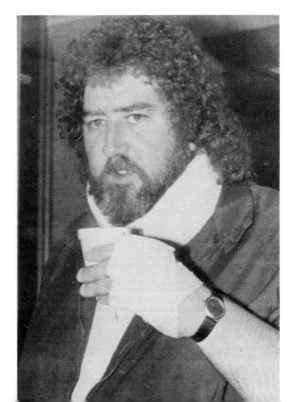

Ron "Bear" Jones was at the wheel of the Odyssey when it was hit from behind. Luckily for Jones, he immediately leaned out of his seat to help Emilio Estefan; if he had not done so, Jones might have been critically injured or killed when the front of the bus caved in.

the driver's side caved in completely. "The space where Bear's head had been a few seconds earlier was now a gaping hole, and although he was pinned helplessly behind the steering wheel, he was still alive," Estefan recalled. So much of the front of the bus had been torn away that snow was now falling inside it.

Gloria was afraid to move. She became aware that she was lying on the floor of the bus, covered with objects that had been thrown around the cabin by the impact of the two crashes. She saw her shaken husband looking anxiously down at her, and she told him, "My back is broken!" He tried to reassure her, reminding her that she had had temporary pain from a pinched nerve in her lower back before. "No, baby, it's okay, you just pulled a muscle," he told her, but Gloria knew from the pain and the tingling sensation in her mouth that this was no ordinary case of her back "going out." Emilio rushed to the back of the bus to check on Nayib, and then came a terrible moment for Gloria: She heard her husband crying and feared that their son was badly injured, or worse. Emilio found the boy lying on the floor, half-buried by an avalanche of purses, books, and bags that had fallen onto him from the bunks and shelves. He was clutching his shoulder—his collarbone was broken—but he was alive and conscious. Emilio had been crying out of relief.

Everyone else in the bus had suffered only minor injuries. Despite her physical agony, Gloria too felt a flood of relief. "With Nayib and Emilio alive," she said, "I knew I could manage whatever else might happen."

Nayib moved forward so he could sit on the couch near his mother and hold her hand. Gloria tried to remain calm, to keep control of herself so that Nayib would believe she was going to be all right. While she talked to her son, she discovered that she could move her feet and legs a little bit. This made her feel better: If she were paralyzed, she reasoned, she would not have had any sensation or been able to move at all. At that moment, a woman who had been in one of the cars that stopped because of the accident came running to the bus and explained that she was a nurse. "Is anyone hurt?" she asked. Gloria said that she thought she had a broken back, and the nurse ordered, "Whatever you do, *don't move!*"

The pain grew worse. Gloria felt one especially sharp pain that seemed to be shooting from her back down into her legs. The skin on her legs became abnormally sensitive—even the touch of a sheet placed over her hurt. As she lay clutching Nayib's hand, she could hear people running and shouting, trying to get help. Then she was told that the nearest hospital was in Scranton, about an hour away, and that it might take two hours for an ambulance to reach the bus because of the traffic jam caused by the accident.

In spite of her determination to be brave, Estefan's eyes filled with tears. She wondered if she would be able to endure the stabbing pain. She wanted to keep on moving her legs a little, just to reassure herself that she was not paralyzed. But she knew that the slightest movement could sever her spinal cord. So she was forced to remain utterly still.

Holding her son's hand, Estefan remembered something she had learned in childbirth classes before Nayib was born—something she thought might help her to cope with the pain. She focused her eyes on a spot on the ceiling and began to concentrate on it, trying not to think about anything. This mental exercise took some of the edge off her pain, but not much. "Believe me, I would rather give birth to 10 kids in a row than go through that kind of pain again," she said later. And she could not empty her mind of what she dreaded most—the thought of being paralyzed, of never being able to move again.

The paramedics arrived almost an hour after the accident. When the first paramedic climbed into the bus and made his way to Estefan, he asked her name. When she told him, he called out to his colleagues, "Oh, my god, we've got a celebrity here!" Estefan asked for painkillers, but the paramedics told her that they could not administer any medication until she had been tested at the

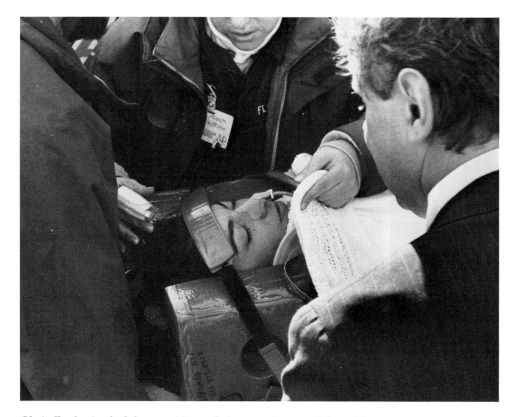

Gloria Estefan is wheeled to a waiting ambulance at the scene of the accident on Highway I-380. Because of a massive traffic jam, paramedics were unable to reach Estefan until an hour after the crash. Estefan was in terrible pain from her broken back, but she had the presence of mind to remain still until help arrived.

hospital: Painkillers might interfere with the doctors' attempts to find out what damage had been done to her back. Then they carefully began to take her out of the bus.

"The pain was almost unbearable as I was strapped to a board and carried through the hole that used to be the windshield," Estefan remembered. "I could feel the snow on my face and see people looking down at me with fear on their faces." She had to be removed through the windshield because the door of the bus was only inches away from a steep slope that was icy and treacherous. The paramedics loaded her into the ambulance as quickly as possible and set off for Scranton with the siren wailing. Estefan fought the pain and told herself over and over that she would make it.

Forty-five minutes later, the ambulance pulled into the Regional Trauma Center of the Scranton Community Medical Center, and Estefan was rushed into the emergency room. Doctors took X rays of her back and then performed computerized axial tomography (also called a CT scan), which provides an image similar to an X ray but more complete. Then, at last, the doctors gave Estefan an injection of morphine to dull the pain. They also told her the results of the examination: Just as she had feared from the first, her back was broken. In that moment, Gloria Estefan faced the possibility that her career might be over forever.

Anti-Castro Cubans taken prisoner after the Bay of Pigs invasion are greeted by their families on their return to Miami, Florida, in December 1962. Gloria Estefan's father was among the returnees, having been held in a Cuban jail since the failure of the invasion in April 1961.

CHAPTER TWO

Cuban Roots

Gloria Estefan was born Gloria María Fajardo in Havana, the capital city of the Caribbean island of Cuba, on September 1, 1957. Her family life and childhood were shaped to a large extent by Cuba's Spanish heritage and by the upheavals that occurred in Cuban politics during the 1950s and 1960s.

Christopher Columbus discovered Cuba during his first voyage to the Americas in 1492. The Spanish, who had sponsored Columbus's expedition, colonized the island and governed it for more than 400 years. The legacy of Spanish rule pervades Cuba's culture to this day: Its people speak Spanish; many Cubans are Roman Catholics; and social life has traditionally followed a Spanish pattern of tightly knit, male-dominated families. Yet, as in most of the Caribbean islands, the many African slaves who were brought to the island by the Spanish over the centuries also contributed enormously to Cuban culture. About 12 percent of Cubans are black, and another 15 percent are of mixed Spanish and African descent. Santería, a religion that melds traditional

An 1898 German cartoon depicts the conflict between Spain and the United States over the island of Cuba. After 400 years of Spanish rule, Cuba gained its independence as a result of the United States's victory in the Spanish-American War. However, the island came under U.S. influence until the Castro revolution in 1959.

Spanish Catholic and African spiritualist elements, is widespread in Cuba. And the Latin music and dance rhythms that appear in the songs of the Miami Sound Machine and other Cuban-American recording artists owe a great deal to Cuba's African musical heritage in addition to Spanish influences.

Cuba gained its independence from Spain in 1898, but for a long time the island was dominated politically and economically by the United States, the southern shore of which lies only 100 miles (160 kilometers) away. In the 1920s, the presidency of Cuba was held by General Geraldo Machado y Morales, whose administration declined into a corrupt and repressive dictatorship. Machado fled the country in 1933, after outbreaks of violent protests and strikes. Suddenly, the most powerful man in Cuba was an army sergeant named Fulgencio Batista y Zaldívar, who was backed by the nation's soldiers. Over the next half-dozen years, four different men were elected president—each with Batista's support—and each was thrown out of office when he failed to meet the demands of Batista and the army. Batista was elected president in 1940, but he left Cuba in 1944 after failing to win reelection. In 1952, however, Batista returned in triumph and, with the help of the still-loyal army, overthrew the government of President Carlos Prío Socarrás; two years later, Batista held a presidential election and declared himself the winner. He took office in 1955.

Batista immediately suspended many of the important constitutional rights that until then had been enjoyed by the Cuban masses: Elections were banned; strict limits were put on speech and political activity; and the press was censored. The denial of what had once been constitutional guarantees was enforced by the state police. Any act of dissent could result in one's arrest, im-

A Cuban exile holds a portait of Fulgencio Batista y Zaldívar (1901–73), the Cuban dictator who was overthrown by Fidel Castro in 1959. The Batista regime was corrupt and repressive, but it enjoyed the support of the U.S. government and the more affluent segments of the Cuban population.

prisonment, and even torture. Though the Batista regime quickly proved to be one of the most corrupt and repressive in the world, the United States gave it official state recognition, prompting Cuba's business class to support the new government whole-heartedly. Soon there was a strong anti-Batista movement through-out the country, and eventually there was an organized armed resistance.

Among the anti-Batista leaders was a lawyer named Fidel Castro. Castro's underground revolutionary group, the 26th of July Movement (named for the unsuccessful raid they conducted against an army barracks in Santiago de Cuba on July 26, 1953), was made up of workers, students, farmers, and others who were anxious to see the corrupt Batista regime fall. In the face of this overwhelming opposition, Batista's tactics grew increasingly severe and oppressive. After 1957, Cuba was torn by civil war as Castro's guerrilla fighters battled Batista's troops in the eastern part of the island.

Gloria Fajardo's family was closely involved in this explosive situation because her father worked for Batista. In his younger days, José Manuel Fajardo had been a championship volleyball player, once winning a medal at the Pan-American Games (an event similar to the Olympics but limited to the nations of North, Central, and South America). At the time of Gloria's birth, he was a motorcycle-mounted bodyguard, part of the army security team that protected the family of the Cuban president. Fajardo's wife, Gloria, was a schoolteacher; the couple's first child was named after her.

The Fajardos lived in Havana and were part of Cuba's growing urban middle class. No doubt they had expected to raise their daughter in comfortable, stable surroundings. But their lives changed suddenly and dramatically in 1959, when Castro, his cohort Ernesto "Che" Guevara, and his band of guerrilla fighters came down from their mountain strongholds and toppled the Batista government.

U.S. television personality Ed Sullivan (left) visits with Cuban rebel leader Fidel Castro in January 1959, shortly after Castro led his troops into Havana and took control of the government. Before long, Castro's left-wing policies alienated both the Cuban middle class and the U.S. government.

Batista fled the country, along with most of his supporters and those who had served in his administration, including many members of the army. Batista went first to the Dominican Republic, on the neighboring island of Hispaniola, and then to Spain, where he died a millionaire in 1973. But hundreds of his friends and followers, called *batistianos*, went to the United States, which was closer to home and which opposed Castro's revolutionary regime almost immediately.

One batistiano who fled was José Manuel Fajardo. Because of his association with the Batista regime, Fajardo knew that nothing good would happen to him or his family in Cuba now that Castro was in power. They arrived in the United States when Gloria—often called Glorita, which means "little Gloria," to distinguish her from her mother—was 16 months old. Long afterward, Gloria Estefan revealed that as a child she was always moved by the popular song "Ferry 'Cross the Mersey," recorded by the British group Gerry & the Pacemakers in the 1960s, because it made her think of the trip her family had made across the sea to their new home.

The Fajardos went first to Texas and then lived briefly in South Carolina. By the time Gloria was about two years old, however, the family had settled in the city that had become the favorite destination for exiles and emigrants from Cuba—Miami, Florida.

Geographically, Miami's location at the southern tip of the Florida peninsula makes it the closest point to Cuba on the U.S. mainland. And the flow of Cuban refugees, political exiles, and immigrants into the city has also made Miami North America's closest point to Cuba culturally. In the years following Castro's

Many businesses owned by Cuban exiles thrive in this section of S.W. 8th Street in Miami, photographed in 1969. As the Castro regime tightened its controls on business activity, more and more enterprising Cubans fled to Miami, settling in an area that came to be known as Little Havana.

takeover, the new Cuban population of Miami transformed a large downtown area of the city into an ethnic district that came to be called Little Havana. Traditional Havana-style shops and cafés lined the streets; the signs and menus were all in Spanish; and, as in Cuba, the sidewalks were dotted with groups of men sipping coffee from vendors' stands while they discussed business, politics, and the events of the day

Unlike many other immigrant groups in American history, the Cuban exiles showed little inclination to assimilate into American society. Most of them believed that Castro's regime would be short-lived and that they would soon be able to return to Cuba. They excitedly planned various schemes for bringing about his downfall. Many of them were willing and eager to do more than just talk, and they soon found an ally in the U.S. government.

Back in Cuba, newspapers were exposing the corruption that had characterized the Batista regime, the crimes his government had committed against the people, and lists of the individuals who had gained financially from his favors. Then, when the mutilated remains of anti-Batista activists who had been tortured to death by his henchmen and hastily buried in unmarked graves were discovered, there was a public outcry for retribution. In response, Castro set out on a plan of "revolutionary justice" that included show trials and executions of former batistianos. Many who were not executed were sentenced to long prison terms. Although the United States had never criticized the atrocities of the Batista regime, it now saw fit to condemn Castro's "revolutionary justice." Castro mockingly pointed out the irony of the new U.S. position of moral outrage against Cuba.

Actually, it was more than the seeking of high moral ground that prompted the United States to condemn Castro's government: The United States opposed Cuba for several reasons. For example, though his 26th of July Movement had originally included all sorts of anti-Batista factions, whatever their individual political beliefs, and was not officially a Communist organization, soon after taking power, Castro announced that Cuba would be governed under Communist principles. He established ties with the Soviet Union and other members of the Communist bloc. Economic reasons also contributed to the U.S. position: After the coup, Castro set out to nationalize—that is, take over on behalf of the nation—millions of dollars' worth of property and businesses in Cuba that had been owned by U.S. companies and individuals. U.S. business interests that had prospered in Cuba during the Batista years—to a large extent because of Batista's willingness to accept money in exchange for favored business status—now found themselves in a position in which not only large profits but millions of dollars in assets could be lost.

The early 1960s were the height of the so-called cold war, as Communist and non-Communist nations built up their armed forces and sought to carve up the world into rival spheres of influence. Following the Cuban revolution, many people in the United States were alarmed to find communism flourishing, so to speak, on their very doorstep. With the encouragement of President John F. Kennedy, the U.S. Central Intelligence Agency (CIA) and the Cuban exile leaders came up with a plan to take back the island. The result was the Bay of Pigs invasion—a political embarrassment for Kennedy, a military disaster for the exiles, and a tragedy for the Fajardo family.

José Manuel Fajardo was one of about 1,300 Cuban exiles who took part in the invasion. They formed a secret military unit called Exile Brigade 2506. Their training, weapons, and other equipment were provided by the CIA. Their plan was to invade Cuba with a swift strike force and knock Castro out of power. On April 17, 1961, Exile Brigade 2506 landed at a place called the Bay of Pigs (Bahia de Cochinos) on Cuba's southwestern coast. The leaders of the invasion force planned to march on Havana and oust Castro. José Manuel Fajardo commanded the brigade's tank division.

Unfortunately for the *brigadistas*, several things went seriously wrong with their plan. They and the United States had counted on massive support from the Cuban population to add a lot of recruits

to their small army. But U.S. intelligence had grossly underes-
timated the extent of Castro's popular support. The Cuban people
in the countryside did not rally to the anti-Castro banner, and
many fought *for* Castro. This blow was accompanied by another
crushing disappointment, one that the Cuban exiles regarded as
a betrayal by their CIA sponsors. U.S. government contacts had
promised that the brigade would receive air cover from U.S. forces—in other words, that U.S. military planes would be present
to protect the brigadistas and to hold off Castro's forces. The
promised air cover never appeared. Once they struggled up the
beaches of the Bay of Pigs, the members of Exile Brigade 2506
were on their own.

No one can say whether the Bay of Pigs invasion would have
succeeded if everything had gone according to plan. As it happened, the invasion was a fiasco. By April 20, it was over. More than
1,100 of the brigadistas were captured by Castro's army. José
Manuel Fajardo was captured by his own cousin, who had taken
Castro's side. Along with the other prisoners, Fajardo was put in
prison and held for ransom by the Castro government, which
demanded that the United States pay for the release of the
brigadistas. Finally, after 18 months of bitter wrangling, the United
States shipped $53 million worth of food and medicine to Cuba,
and Castro in turn released the members of Exile Brigade 2506.
Fajardo and the others were returned to the United States a few
days before Christmas, 1962.

While Gloria's father was preparing for his part in the Bay of
Pigs invasion, her mother was establishing the family in its new
home. The Fajardos—along with many other Cuban families who
were newly arrived in Miami—had settled in the area of the city
located behind the Orange Bowl football stadium. This neighborhood of large, barrackslike apartment buildings quickly took on
a Cuban flavor, which remained unchanged into the 1990s.

The Fajardos had little money when they arrived in the United
States, making their transition to a new life in a new country even
more difficult. Other problems arose out of language barriers and

A Cuban exile works on a political pamphlet. With so many men imprisoned after the Bay of Pigs invasion, Cuban-American women often had to go to work while coping with a foreign culture. Gloria Fajardo helped her mother learn English so that she could qualify for a Florida teacher's license.

prejudice. Although the United States, and Miami in particular, had seen its share of Latin American tourists and even a few immigrants over the years, the exiles who fled after Castro's takeover formed the first large wave of Hispanic political refugees to hit U.S. shores. Many of them were broke, and few of them spoke English. As a group, these refugees were not welcomed with open arms by the Anglo, or white, community.

Gloria Estefan later recalled that her whole family was deeply affected by what she termed the "political trauma" of the Bay of Pigs: "I don't remember much about Cuba, but I do remember my first years here. . . . I was alone in America with my mother while my father was in jail in Cuba." The failure of the Bay of Pigs invasion meant that the Cuban exile community experienced a difficult start in Miami. Many of the men were absent, leaving the women and children to fend for themselves. Like most of the Cuban women and children, neither Gloria nor her mother spoke

English. "In Miami there was a lot of prejudice at the time," Estefan said. "It was a very difficult time because it was the South, . . . all these Hispanics coming into one place that had never had any Hispanics at all. It was difficult. I remember that my mom had a really tough time dealing with it."

Life in a new country was not easy for Gloria, either. She had just begun to learn English by the time she started school. On the first day of first grade, she found that she was the only Hispanic student in her class. Inevitably she felt like an outsider, different from the other students and not able to communicate well in their language. But even at this young age she showed a trait that she demonstrated over and over again throughout her life—her willingness to throw herself head-on at any obstacle or difficulty and work as hard as necessary to overcome it.

Mastering English became an exciting and fascinating challenge for Gloria. She enjoyed it so much that she won an award for her reading skills—in English—just six months after starting school. As she developed her love of language, she began to write poetry and helped teach her mother English. She also studied French and learned to speak it fluently. In college, she studied communications and worked part-time as a translator. Later, she wrote many of the Miami Sound Machine's hit ballads and won respect for her songwriting abilities. As it turned out, her Spanish remained at a rather basic level—"very simple, very conversational," in her words—because high school policy prevented her from taking courses in her native language. Because she had used English most of the time since her early childhood, her adopted language became her main means of expression.

While she was growing up, Gloria was as interested in music as she was in language. Songs and singing were always a part of her life, thanks to the influence of her mother and grandmother, who both loved music. Gloria's mother had enjoyed singing ever since her own childhood. In fact, as a youngster she came close to having a show business career of her own. In 1940, she entered a talent contest held to find a Spanish-speaking girl whose voice could be dubbed into the movies of Shirley Temple, a popular child star of the day. Gloria's mother won the contest. However, Gloria's grandfather was somewhat old-fashioned and did not like the idea of his young daughter going off to Hollywood to work in the movie industry, so the honor of being the "Spanish Shirley Temple" went to someone else.

But Gloria's mother continued to sing and to listen to records and the radio, and she shared this passion for music with her own family. As a child, Gloria spent hours listening to her mother's collection of records. Her favorites were ballads—simple, emotional songs in both English and Spanish. She remembers singing along to the tunes of balladeers such as Agustín Lara, Jorge Negrete, and Johnny Mathis. "But my big idol, the big crush of my life," she recalled, "was Joselito, this little child actor who sang in Spanish." When Gloria was a little older, in her teen years, her favorite singers were Barbra Streisand and Diana Ross; throughout her career, she continued to list Ross as one of the people she most admired.

The first stage of Estefan's musical education, the simple love of music in two languages, was something that she had inherited effortlessly from her mother. The formal phase of her training began later. At the insistence of her parents, she began taking lessons in classical guitar, a type of music that has traditionally been associated with Spanish composers and performers. Although she was naturally musical, Gloria did not enjoy her guitar lessons. "I hated it," she stated bluntly. "It really turned me off, because music is like a language to me. To sit down and say 'This note is this' seemed to take all the fun out of it. It was really tedious, and I wished I could just sit down and play."

Like many music students before and since, Gloria was impatient with the slow pace and organized structure of her lessons. Before long, though, she had become a good enough guitar player to begin strumming her favorite ballads and the popular songs she

President John F. Kennedy receives the battle flag of Brigade 2506 at a ceremony in Miami's Orange Bowl in December 1962. Despite Kennedy's tribute to the brigadistas, many of them felt that the U.S. government had betrayed them by not providing enough support during the Bay of Pigs invasion.

heard on the radio. Her playing and singing came to occupy a very important and very private part of her life during her high school years, when she was troubled and lonely.

Part of Estefan's unhappiness as a teenager was due to a family tragedy. Although her father had been reunited with the family a year and a half after the Bay of Pigs, the failure of the invasion galled him and the other brigadistas. The exiles never stopped dreaming and plotting, always hoping to go back to Cuba someday. In the meantime, however, they had to find a way to earn a living in the United States. Many of the Exile Brigade 2506 veterans were career soldiers like Gloria's father, and it seemed natural for them to enlist in the U.S. Army. José Manuel Fajardo took this path.

In the army, Fajardo quickly rose to the rank of captain and then volunteered for duty in Vietnam, where the United States was becoming deeply embroiled in a war with Communist guerrillas and the North Vietnamese troops. Gloria later explained that her father had by no means given up the idea of a victorious return to Cuba: "He felt that if he did this [fought in Vietnam], then later on he could ask the U.S. for help to try Cuba again." But there was to be no second chance at Cuba for José Manuel Fajardo.

Fajardo returned from 2 years of duty in Vietnam in 1968, when Gloria was 10 years old. Before long, family and friends noticed that something was wrong with him. "He'd fall for no reason," Gloria remembered. "Or he'd stop for a red light, but the light would be green." Gloria's mother insisted that her husband go into the hospital for tests. By the time the tests were finished and

U.S. military aircraft spray Agent Orange defoliant over a Vietnamese jungle in 1966. When José Manuel Fajardo contracted multiple sclerosis shortly after returning from service in Vietnam, his doctors believed that exposure to Agent Orange might have been the cause of the disease.

Fajardo was allowed to go home, he needed a cane in order to walk. The doctors determined that he had multiple sclerosis (MS), a disease that affects the brain and spinal cord. MS often produces muscle tremors and generally leads to paralysis. Some time later, the family learned that while Fajardo was in Vietnam he had been exposed to Agent Orange, a chemical used by the U.S. military to strip leaves from trees in areas where enemy forces were believed to have been hiding. After the war, medical researchers linked Agent Orange with cancer and other diseases suffered by U.S. veterans. Fajardo's doctors believed that his exposure to the chemical may have been the cause of his illness.

Fajardo's MS had a drastic effect on his family. The former athlete and soldier was soon bedridden, unable to care for himself. By this time, Gloria's mother had learned English and was working all day and going to school at night. Eventually, she had her Cuban teacher's credentials recertified in English, so that she could teach in a Miami school. This improved the family finances, but it meant that Gloria's mother was kept away from home a lot by her busy schedule. As a result, much of the burden of caring for her invalid father fell on young Gloria's shoulders.

"I took care of Dad from the time I was 11 until I was 16," Estefan recalled. Every day, she came home from school and did what needed to be done around the house. In addition to taking care of her father, she was also responsible for looking after her younger sister, Rebecca, called Becky for short.

The responsibilities she carried at home did not keep Gloria from doing well in school. She was an honor student at the all-girl Catholic high school she attended. But tending to her father and witnessing his steady, irreversible decline weighed heavily on Gloria. As Fajardo's condition worsened, he became unable to feed or clean himself, and Gloria had to perform these and other tasks for him. She knew that her father was ashamed of his dependence upon her, and her heart ached for him—and for herself. Estefan later reflected, "I looked so much older [as a teenager] than I do now because I was carrying the weight of the whole world on my shoulders. I was used to being so full of responsibility, never being able to let go because I was afraid to. I was handling a lot, trying to be strong for my mom, and I was kind of like my sister's mom. . . . I felt really alone in my life. It was a situation that I could see no way of getting out of."

Throughout these difficult years, Estefan kept her feelings of loneliness to herself and did not complain. Her sister, Becky Fajardo, later described Estefan's strong sense of self-control: "She's iron, iron on the outside. When something is bothering her, it doesn't show. I've seen her cry maybe once."

Even when she was alone in her room, Gloria did not give way to tears. "I would not cry," she said. "I was afraid if I let go just a little bit, it would all go." During this period in her life, music became more than a hobby. It became her way of crying, of expressing her emotional side. "When my father was ill, music was my escape. It was my release from everything. I'd lock myself up in my room with my guitar. . . . I would sing for hours by myself." Back then, Gloria sang other people's songs—Top 40 tunes she heard on the radio and ballads she had learned from her mother—but those years of expressing her feelings through song formed the basis for her later success as a writer and singer of her own ballads.

Gloria's father grew steadily worse. When she was 16 years old, his condition was so bad that he had to be moved to a Veterans Administration hospital. A big responsibility was lifted from Gloria's shoulders, but her life did not change overnight. She still had to help her mother take care of the house and Becky; she started giving guitar lessons to earn a little money; and she continued to put in a lot of time studying in order to remain an honor student—an effort that paid off when she was awarded a partial scholarship to the University of Miami.

Gloria did not have much of a social life as a teenager, and she later admitted that her father's illness was not the only reason for this: Like many adolescents, she was very shy and considered herself something of a loner. In high school, she recalled, she was so quiet, timid, and well behaved that the nuns who were her teachers thought she would probably become a nun herself. (If any of these nuns later watched MTV, they must have been surprised to recognize their demure former student Gloria Fajardo in the lively, racy videos featuring Gloria Estefan.)

In addition, Gloria was not confident about her looks—another feeling shared by many teenagers. She was five feet one inch tall, with the same wavy dark brown hair and glowing dark eyes that her fans later came to admire, but she was not as slim and shapely as she later became. She was, in fact, chubby. So although Gloria did occasionally play the guitar and sing in school concerts, her shyness kept her out of the spotlight for most of her teenage years. But her transformation from a shy, plump wallflower to a dazzling superstar began in 1975, when she met the man who was to become her partner—first in music and later in marriage.

The name of this Cuban restaurant expresses the attitude of many Cuban exiles: For them, Cuba existed only in its transplanted form in Miami. When Emilio Estefan reached Miami in 1967, at the age of 13, he found a thriving Cuban community and an opportunity to fulfill his ambitions.

CHAPTER THREE

Emilio and the Latin Boys

Emilio Estefan, Jr., founded the Miami Sound Machine, and many people in the music industry considered him the person most responsible for the group's success. Although he stopped performing with MSM in 1987, he continued to produce all of its records—that is, to create or approve all of the musical arrangements and supervise the blending of soundtracks in the studio to produce the final sound. During more than a decade of nonstop effort, he changed MSM from a local band practicing in a garage to a world-famous act with Gloria Estefan at center stage.

Emilio Estefan was also born in Cuba, five years before Gloria Fajardo. His parents had emigrated from Lebanon, at the eastern end of the Mediterranean Sea. They settled in Santiago de Cuba, the second-largest city on the island, where they started an underwear factory. Like the Fajardo family, the Estefans fled Cuba after the revolution.

Gloria retained few memories of her childhood in Cuba because she was only a toddler when she left the island. Emilio, on the other hand, was seven years old when Castro took over in 1959; in addition, his family did not leave Cuba at once, as the Fajardos had. Instead, the Estefans remained in Cuba for six more years, reluctant to leave their home and hopeful of saving their business. One of the principles of Castro's regime, however, was that property should not be privately owned. Under his leadership, the state gradually took control of farms, stores, and factories throughout the island, including the Estefans' plant.

When Emilio was 13, he and his father left Cuba. His older brother, José, was unable to accompany them because he had reached the age when he was eligible to be drafted into the Cuban army, and the government did not permit young men of draft age to emigrate.

Emilio and his father went to Madrid, Spain, where they began the time-consuming process of applying for visas (entry permits) to the United States. Almost two years later, in 1967, Emilio arrived in Miami—penniless but armed with a student visa. From that point on, his story is the classic tale of a youthful immigrant who works hard to send money to his relatives overseas while building a life for himself in his new country.

Upon arriving in Miami, Estefan moved into a small apartment with 15 of his aunts and cousins. He spoke little English at the time, but he immediately set out, with typical energy and determination, to adapt himself to life in America—and above all, to find a way of earning money so that he could bring other members of his family to the United States.

Estefan worked at odd jobs wherever he could find them. People liked him and wanted to help him out because he was a good talker—a quality that later opened many doors for MSM in the recording industry. He was also a natural-born entrepreneur, someone who creates a business by seeing what people need and finding a way to provide it. After he learned how to drive, for example, he obtained a beat-up Volkswagen and used it to run errands for the elderly Cuban women in his neighborhood. He would ferry them to and from the grocery store in return for whatever change they felt like giving him. Later, he started a small T-shirt business. His most unusual idea, though, involved beauty pageants, which are highly popular in the Miami area. Using ribbons from old funeral wreaths, Estefan manufactured the sashes worn by contestants in the pageants.

In 1968, Estefan got a job as a mail clerk in the offices of Bacardi Imports, a company that distills and markets rum, a liquor made from fermented sugarcane and produced chiefly in the Caribbean region. The story of the young man who starts out in the mail room and rises to an executive position in the company is a tired old cliché of American business. But in Emilio Estefan's case, that is exactly what happened. He impressed his superiors, who promoted him rapidly. Twelve years after going to work at Bacardi, Emilio became the company's director of Latin marketing.

As he was just beginning his climb up the corporate ladder at Bacardi, Estefan was also putting his musical skills to work. Like Gloria Fajardo, he had loved music from a very early age, even though he did not come from a musical family. When he was six years old, Estefan received an accordion as a Christmas gift. Although he had no formal training, he soon taught himself to play the instrument, and he even formed a small band with several of his friends before leaving Cuba.

Once he was settled in Miami, Estefan decided to take up music again, this time as a business. First, he went to a music store and bargained with the owner for a good price on a secondhand accordion. Then he approached the owner of an Italian restaurant on Miami's elegant Biscayne Boulevard and offered to play for free, relying on whatever tips he could get. Without further preparation, he launched his career as a musical soloist, entertaining diners at the restaurant with tunes he had taught himself. His repertoire included a variety of material, ranging from Cuban dance music to Italian-American favorites such as "Volare" to party standards such as "The Beer Barrel Polka."

The restaurant patrons must have liked Estefan and his accordion because he was soon playing there regularly and earning a respectable amount in tips. His boss at Bacardi heard of this musical enterprise and asked Estefan to entertain at a party he was giving. Estefan knew that this was an important opportunity to take

Cuban-American bandleader Desi Arnaz, who later starred as Ricky Ricardo in the popular television show "I Love Lucy," appears in the 1949 movie musical Holiday in Havana. *Arnaz was one of several performers who brought Cuba's rich musical heritage to the United States: Others included Pérez Prado, Xavier Cugat, and Celia Cruz.*

a big step forward as a musician; if he did a good job at this engagement, the party guests in turn would hire him or recommend him to friends.

Estefan decided that he needed some help. A lone accordion might be enough to keep people happy while they ate dinner, but it would probably not do the trick for partygoers who wanted to dance and enjoy themselves for hours. So he brought along a drummer and a conga player. (The conga is a tall, narrow drum played with the hands rather than with drumsticks; it is a traditional Cuban instrument with African roots and is very similar to drums used throughout Africa.)

Estefan's first venture into party entertainment was a definite success. He and his two fellow musicians played for nine hours. The party guests were Cubans, so the group relied on two types of Cuban songs. The first were boleros, rhythmic, repetitive songs to which dancers move in sharp turns, with abrupt halts and much stamping of the feet. Then there were congas, African-Cuban songs featuring a strong beat on the conga drums; conga dancers line up in single file and move forward in a series of three steps followed by a synchronized kick.

Just as Estefan had hoped, playing at that first party led to other engagements. Word of his combo spread, and requests for his services started flowing in. He soon decided to expand the group so that they could play more kinds of music—and therefore get more jobs. He added guitars, keyboards, and a horn section. By

1974, he had organized a nine-member band, which he called the Miami Latin Boys. They practiced in the crowded one-car garage at his aunt's house. Around that time, Estefan began acting on occasion as the group's percussionist, dropping the accordion and swinging over to the drums or other rhythm instruments.

The Estefan family initially tried to discourage Emilio from becoming too involved in performing. They felt that he should concentrate on building a stable business career and that the music business was too uncertain. "Everybody told me I was crazy," he recalled. "My parents told me that music wasn't the right thing to do, it wasn't very secure, but I said that's what I like to do and that's what I want to do. They eventually came around and were supportive of me."

The Miami Latin Boys were a pleasant and fairly successful musical ensemble, if not a very distinctive one. Carlos Oliva, a Miami bandleader who managed the group in the mid-1970s, recalled: "They were a soft, mellow group to begin with—and not very exciting to watch." Rather than trying to become a dramatic and original act, the Latin Boys played the same tunes that a hundred other part-time bands used, and they performed them in the same way. They were not trying to make a name for themselves as creative artists; rather, they were simply trying to earn some cash and have some fun playing what their audiences expected to hear.

The Latin Boys found steady work at private parties, weddings, bar mitzvahs, and *quinces* (coming-out parties that are traditionally given for Latin American girls when they turn 15). In short, the band was talented and hardworking but decidedly ordinary—or, as a writer for *Rolling Stone* magazine described them in 1990, "a profitable little weekend business, nothing to quit your day job for."

But Emilio Estefan was not content to remain at that level. In 1975, he began making some changes in the Miami Latin Boys— first in the membership of the band, then in its name, and finally in its sound. The most important change of all brought Gloria Fajardo onto the bandstand.

Members of the Martí Theater ride a float during Miami's Three Kings Parade in January 1988. When the Miami Latin Boys was formed in the mid-1970s, Cuban-American bands were all-male. Emilio Estefan decided that the addition of female singers would make his group unique; he asked Gloria Fajardo and her cousin Merci to join the band.

CHAPTER FOUR

MSM Is Born

Gloria Fajardo first saw Emilio Estefan in 1975, when her high school invited him, as the leader of a band, to speak to the music students. A short while later, she and several of her girlfriends were putting together a musical group to entertain the guests at a party that their parents were arranging. The father of one of Gloria's friends worked at Bacardi and knew Estefan; he asked the young musician to help the girls get started. "They brought Emilio over to give us some pointers on putting a band together because he already had a band," Gloria recalled. "Anyway, he heard me sing there and that was it." If her singing made any particular impression on him at that time, it was something that he kept to himself.

Fajardo and Estefan met for the third time at a big Cuban wedding. The Miami Latin Boys were on hand to provide the entertainment, which consisted of salsa, a characteristically Cuban type of upbeat, fast-moving dance music. Gloria remembered that she did not really want to go to the wedding: "My mother had to drag me to it."

During the festivities, Gloria got an insight into Estefan's personality. "Here was this guy at this Latin wedding performing with his band," she reminisced, "and you knew he was gutsy because he would play all this salsa stuff and all of a sudden he would start playing 'Do the Hustle' on the accordion." She admired Estefan's willingness to surprise his audience, to take a chance on upsetting them with something unexpected, and even to risk looking foolish. She liked his bold, confident style, perhaps because she herself was shy and withdrawn.

Gloria remembered meeting Estefan before, and as she recalls it, "We ran into each other during the band's break and he immediately recognized me. He approached me and asked if I would sing a couple of numbers with the band for fun." Fajardo was not enthusiastic about the idea at first, but Estefan would not take no for an answer. In addition, Fajardo's mother was eager to hear her sing. Fajardo finally gave in.

She remembered that the band "hated it" when Estefan told them that a complete unknown was going to sit in for a few songs. Such occasions are most often a source of embarrassment and irritation for band members, who have the unwelcome task of making an inexperienced and often untalented amateur look good in front of family and friends. In this case, however, Estefan already knew that Fajardo was talented, and he wanted to try her out with the group. He assured them, "Don't worry. I've heard her sing. She can handle it."

The Miami Latin Boys discovered that Gloria could, indeed, handle it. She sang several of her mother's favorite Cuban ballads. Many of her mother's old friends were there, and Gloria's performance earned her a standing ovation. She had found the experience of singing with the band highly enjoyable.

At the time, the Latin Boys did not have a lead singer. Estefan and the other members of the band would take turns singing, or they would all sing together. Not long before, the Latin Boys had acquired two new members, both of them students about Gloria

Fajardo's age. Juan Marcos Avila played bass guitar, and Enrique Garcia, called Kiki, played the drums. After hearing Fajardo sing at the wedding, Estefan decided that the band definitely needed a singer—a female singer.

A few weeks after the wedding, in October 1975, Estefan called Fajardo and invited her to join the band. Estefan always had a gift for recognizing a good angle or a promising marketing idea. He realized that having a woman as a lead singer would give his band a different and memorable quality, something to set it apart from the dozens of similar all-male groups that were performing around Miami.

At first, Fajardo dismissed the idea. She was just getting started at the University of Miami and did not want to be distracted from her studies. She told Estefan that she was too busy with school to join a band. But Estefan did not give up easily. He called again two weeks later, and this time he assured Fajardo that singing with the band would not interfere with her college work. Performing would be "like a hobby," he told her; the group would expect her to sing only on weekends and during vacations. "Well, I loved music so much that I couldn't let a great opportunity like this pass me by," Gloria later confessed. She agreed to join.

Before she did anything, however, the 18-year-old student had to get her family's permission. That was the way things were done in close-knit Cuban families. Fajardo's mother and grandmother asked some questions about Estefan and his fellow musicians and finally decided that it would be all right for Gloria to associate with these young men.

Gloria's cousin Merci was also interested in singing with the Latin Boys. Estefan told them both to come over to his aunt's garage, where the group was still practicing. Then he phoned Carlos Oliva, who was then the band's manager. "He told me I better come over to rehearsal at his aunt's house," Oliva remembered. "He said there was this girl he met at a wedding, and she was coming by to audition with her cousin. . . . I got there late, and there in the middle of all these neighbors was Gloria and her cousin Merci, harmonizing. It was beautiful!" Two weeks later, Fajardo found herself at the Dupont Plaza Hotel in Miami, singing "What a Diff'rence a Day Makes" and playing maracas, dried gourds that are filled with seeds or pebbles and shaken in time to the music.

Once Fajardo stopped worrying about finding time for both music and school, she began to fully enjoy her time with the band. For a young woman who had had almost no social life throughout high school, becoming part of Miami's music scene was exhilarating. As she remembered it, "All of a sudden I was going to parties every weekend, singing with a whole band behind me, making money for it, and enjoying every second."

Fajardo did not let the excitement go to her head or change her values, however. She remained the same hardworking, basically serious person she had always been. She stayed in school, where she majored in communications and psychology and earned A's in most of her courses. She also put her language skills to work by serving as a part-time translator for the U.S. Customs Bureau at Miami International Airport. (The Customs Bureau is responsible for supervising the arrival of passengers and goods from other countries.) On top of everything else, she gave guitar lessons at a community center.

With the addition of Gloria and Merci Fajardo, the Miami Latin Boys had to make some adjustments. For one thing, the name of the band was no longer accurate. One of Estefan's advisers suggested "Miami Sound Machine," but Fajardo never liked the name. "It was the beginning of the disco era, and 'machine' seemed to be a common name," she later remarked. "In my mind, a machine didn't have anything to do with what we were." The new name stuck, however, and many people liked it—*People* magazine, for example, called it "a catchy, unusual name."

The other adjustment that the band made after Fajardo joined concerned the music it performed. Previously, the Latin Boys had played two kinds of music, depending on the occasion. For audiences of Cubans or other Hispanics, they specialized in Latin American dance music, particularly salsa. For Anglo audiences, they played middle-of-the-road rock music favorites, Top 40 hits, and mainstream pop standards. They did not perform original material, and they did not use ballads in their act.

When she joined the band, Fajardo was not familiar with salsa, but she knew a lot of pop songs and a lot of ballads. She felt that she added something to the band's musical style, and at the same time, she learned something about salsa and Latin dance music. She was not the only newcomer to the band who had to learn salsa:

Tito Puente and Celia Cruz—shown here during Puente's enshrinement in the Hollywood Walk of Fame in 1990—were universally considered the king and queen of salsa. Salsa, a blend of Latin American dance music with jazz and rock, was new to Gloria Fajardo when she joined the Miami Latin Boys.

When Kiki Garcia joined the Latin Boys he was, as he put it, "heavy into disco." In order to learn the music that the band played at parties, Garcia went to a record store and stocked up on records by Tito Puente and Celia Cruz, universally recognized as the top salsa artists. Over time, the different musical styles and influences shared by the band's members merged into MSM's distinctive sound. A decade after Fajardo joined the group, their unusual combination of gentle, sensitive ballads and fast-moving, foot-kicking Latin dance tunes propelled MSM to stardom.

Gloria Estefan performs with the Miami Sound Machine during a concert in Tokyo, Japan. Although she joined the band in 1975 and married Emilio Estefan (far left) in 1978, Gloria did not emerge as the lead singer until 1982. During those seven years, she worked hard to improve her singing and overcome her shyness.

"Our sound evolved from trying to please all the people," explained Juan Marcos Avila, the bass player. "Here in Miami, we have Cubans, Anglos, blacks, South Americans. You have to be very versatile." This versatility made it possible for MSM to play at a wide variety of events and made them the band of choice for those who wanted different styles of music but did not want to pay two bands. Of course, it also meant that MSM had to work twice as hard, but all the members of the band were prepared to put in overtime. They took as many jobs as they could line up, sometimes playing at three or even four weddings or quinces in one night.

Emilio Estefan's hunch about adding Gloria and Merci Fajardo to his combo proved to be correct. Just a few months after they joined the group, MSM was the leading party band in Miami. But Gloria was not yet front and center, in the spotlight. She sang, but much of the time she remained somewhat in the background. "When I first joined," she recalled, "it was because I loved music, not because I wanted to perform. I didn't want to be in the spotlight, didn't desire it. . . . It never crossed my mind that this is what I'd do the rest of my life. I wanted to be a psychologist." Gradually, though, she found herself becoming more involved with the group, and she started to think of herself as a performer, struggling to overcome the self-consciousness that held her back. "I loved it more and more, and little by little it just started coming out more. I was very shy, and it was a painful process for me. I didn't really get to the forefront of the band until 1982." The seven years between her introduction to MSM and her emergence as its lead singer were filled with hard work. They also brought the blossoming of a romance.

Gloria and Emilio Estefan relax at their Miami home. The couple's emotional involvement grew slowly because they were afraid of ruining their professional relationship. They dated for two years before deciding to get married.

CHAPTER FIVE

Latin Superstars

The relationship between Gloria Fajardo and Emilio Estefan cannot be described as a case of love at first sight. Instead, like their professional success, it developed over time. From the start, Fajardo was drawn to Estefan, but she was convinced that he could not possibly return her feelings. At 23, he was 5 years older than she, and, she recalled, he "had a reputation as a womanizer," adding that this "turned out not to be true at all." At that time, Estefan was dating women in their thirties; Fajardo doubted that he would be interested in an unsophisticated college freshman. Gloria's sister, Becky, remembered what Estefan was like in those days: "Emilio was the catch of the town. Handsome, driving around in his Corvette. . . . He'd rub so much leather cleaner into those seats that you'd slide forward every time he hit the brakes!"

Although his busy social life continued after Gloria Fajardo joined the band, Estefan did find his new singer attractive. "The moment when I first met her, I thought she had beautiful skin, beautiful eyes," he remembered. "But love is something that grows.

And I remember I told my mother, 'I am not going to make a move on this girl unless I am serious. She's been through too much.'"

From October 1975 until July 1976, Fajardo and Estefan worked together without acknowledging the growing attraction they felt. "He would always flirt with me, but he flirts with *everybody* . . . that's his personality," Gloria maintained. She enjoyed the flirtation, but at the same time she was concerned that if a romantic relationship developed and ended badly, their partnership in the band would be ruined. "It's funny," she added, "because I found out later that he was thinking the same thing. We would've been screwing up two things: our own personal lives and a good working relationship. The attraction was there but we wanted to be very careful. Little by little our relationship grew."

July 4, 1976, was the bicentennial of the Declaration of Indepenedence. Festivals, celebrations, and parties were held all over the United States. In Miami, the Sound Machine was booked to play at an event being held on a ship. After finishing one set of songs, Fajardo and Estefan went up onto the deck for some fresh air. "He kept telling me it was his birthday," Gloria recalled. "Well, he was lying. His birthday was really in March." Teasingly, Estefan told her that she owed him a birthday kiss because she had not got him a present. Finally, he persuaded her to kiss him. What started out as a peck on the cheek turned into a serious kiss. After that, the two began dating, letting their relationship grow slowly. "We dated for two years before we even thought about marriage," Estefan recalled. "I liked her, but I wanted to be sure. I thought, 'If she's in love with me, and I'm not ready, she will be destroyed.'"

During those two years of dating, Fajardo began a process of transforming herself, reshaping her looks through diet and exercise. According to Becky Fajardo, much of her sister's motivation to lose weight and improve her appearance came from Estefan. "He'd always be saying to Gloria, 'I think you can improve yourself 95 percent.' All the time—'*noventa y cinco por ciento.*'"

Fajardo reacted with resentment. She would respond: "If you think I could improve myself 95 percent, then why are you with

Fajardo launched a rigorous exercise program when she began dating Emilio Estefan. At first she resented his insistence that she could improve herself "95 percent," but eventually she realized that he wanted her to feel better about her appearance and be more self-assertive.

me? You only like 5 percent of me?" Soon, however, she understood what he was getting at. "Emilio just meant I could come out of myself more. I used to kid him after that: 'Okay, what am I down to? Seventy-five percent? Sixty?'" While she was shedding pounds, Fajardo was also overcoming her shyness, starting to dress more attractively and act more assertively. "When I was shy, I felt I had something in me I wanted to bring out, I just didn't know how to do it," she said later. "It was a painful process, but I forced myself to do it, mostly by watching myself on videotape, which is the most horrendous experience there is. But it's the only way you can see what other people are seeing." She felt that Estefan's confidence in her was helping her realize her potential: "Emilio saw a side of me that I didn't let people see, and he wanted that to come out."

While keeping up with MSM's performance schedule, Estefan continued to work at Bacardi, and Fajardo pursued her studies at the University of Miami, from which she graduated in 1978 with a B.A. in psychology and communications. That same year, the couple announced their engagement. They were married several months later, on September 1, 1978. Ironically, the couple who had first performed together at a wedding and had provided the music for hundreds more did not have a band at their own wedding. They did not even have a party. "We had saved some money," Gloria recalled, "but we decided to spend it on a trip to Japan instead of a reception. Emilio said we should take the time now to go on a vacation together, because we may never have the chance again."

In addition to graduating from college and getting married, in 1978 Gloria Estefan made her only visit to Cuba since her parents fled with her to the United States. The visit centered around José Estefan, Emilio's older brother, who had remained in Cuba when the rest of the Estefan family left in the mid-1960s. In 1978, José decided that he was ready to leave Cuba along with his own family. But he needed help. The Castro regime frowned upon emigration, and Cubans who sought to leave the island often had great difficulty in doing so. When the authorities learned that the Estefans had made arrangements to go within two months, they put a great deal of pressure on the family. "Their life was made very difficult and reprisals at work and school made them go into hiding until the day of their flight," Gloria recalled. "We had to take them clothing and food to live on for the two months."

This trip to Cuba was a chance for Gloria to see the homeland about which she had heard so many stories while she was growing up. It was also her introduction to life in a Communist country, and the experience reinforced her strong opposition to communism. "For me there was an overwhelming claustrophobic feeling while I was there," she said. "It made me very sad." Years later, this trip produced some political repercussions because of the strong feelings that Castro's Cuba arouses among Cuban exiles in the United States.

The idea of returning to Cuba is a highly emotional issue to many Cuban Americans, especially those living in Miami. Thirty years after Castro's takeover, the political climate in Miami's Little Havana remained overwhelmingly anti-Castro. The Cuban-American community often reacted with hostility to anyone who appeared to support or even tolerate Castro.

Visits to Cuba were an important matter in this political climate because in the first years of *el exilio*, most of the exiles had vowed that they would never set foot in Cuba as long as Castro remained in power. They felt that to return to Cuba, even briefly, would be a concession to Castro. They preferred to remember Cuba as it had been for them before Castro; for many of them, Cuba ceased to exist when they left it—except in its transplanted form in Miami, where many of the streets and public parks bear the same names as those in Havana and Santiago de Cuba. Because anti-Castro feeling among the Cuban exiles remained so strong, more recent Cuban refugees and Cuban Americans who maintained their connection with the island were sometimes regarded with suspicion by other Cuban Americans in the United States.

In the spring of 1989, nearly 11 years after the Estefans' trip to Cuba, questions about the trip were raised in the press. The questions stemmed from an incident at that year's Calle Ocho Festival, an annual musical and cultural event held on Calle Ocho (8th Street), in the heart of Little Havana. Some performers were boycotted by Cuban Americans who claimed that they had ties to Castro's government or that they had performed in Cuba.

The boycott did not affect MSM, but an article in the *Chicago Tribune* suggested that the Estefans had kept their 1978 trip to Cuba a secret in order to avoid any problems in Miami. As soon as she saw the newspaper column, Gloria wrote to the *Tribune* to set the record straight. "Whenever I've been asked if I have ever been back to Cuba," she wrote, "I have always been very open about my experience. I've enlightened some people who have never been to Cuba as to the realities of living in a communist country." She was both surprised and saddened by the column, feeling that the facts about her trip to Cuba on family business had been twisted to make a political point.

Politics has always been an intensely personal subject for Gloria Estefan. "I do have my opinions about politics," she indicated, "but it has been so interwoven into my personal life that I have always tried to keep politics out of my music. Music to me has always been my one escape from everything that was happening. For some people, it's good to be writers who can express their political views through their music but . . . personally it's not my thing. Love and emotions are things that everyone can share, but politics and religion can get you into a lot of trouble." She has said many times that she makes music for her own pleasure and that of her audiences, not in the service of any particular set of ideas. "What I say is not going to affect anyone or change anything. My business is not that—my business is to try to evoke emotion." And although she remained extremely proud of her Hispanic heritage, she always refused to get involved in the volatile world of Cuban-American exile politics: "I don't want people to want me to champion their cause."

Although Estefan was not politically active, the Cuban government understood her anti-Castro position quite well. In 1987,

Estefan performs at the Pan-American Games in Indianapolis, Indiana, in 1987. Because of her father's involvement in the Bay of Pigs invasion, Estefan's appearance at the Games was protested by the Cuban government.

when the Pan-American Games—the competition in which Gloria's father had once won a gold medal—were being held in Indianapolis, Indiana, MSM was among the performers scheduled to appear at the event. The delegation of Cuban athletes protested the booking of MSM and threatened to walk out of the competition if the group performed. In the end, MSM played as scheduled, the Cuban athletes remained in Indianapolis, and the fuss subsided without incident. Estefan pointed out that she and the group did not intend to make a political statement by appearing at the Games—the statement consisted of what other people chose to read into their presence.

Estefan made it clear to everyone that even though a number of her songs had been hits in Cuba, she would never perform on the island as long as Castro was in power. To do so, she once told her bosses at CBS Records, would be a betrayal of her father, a slap in his face. "It would be the ultimate insult to our heritage if we performed [in Cuba]. We cannot return."

During the late 1970s, MSM continued to grow in popularity in the Miami area. The Estefans and their fellow musicians were the reigning local band for parties, and they also played in dance clubs, performing a mix of Latin dance music and Top 40–style pop tunes that were often sung in Spanish if the audience was mostly Hispanic. Emilio decided that it was time for MSM to take the next step and reach a larger audience. The way to accomplish that was through recordings.

Beginning in 1978, MSM recorded a series of three albums, the first on a small local label that specialized in Latin music and the second and third on their own label. Each of these records featured songs in both English and Spanish, with the English songs on one side and the Spanish songs on the other. The songs were recorded and produced in small studios on very low budgets—according to a 1990 article in *Rolling Stone* magazine, MSM's first album cost only $2,000 to produce, a far cry from the lavish budgets of rock superstars today. The material was a mixture of

Cuban standards, disco-style pop music, and ballads, some of which Gloria wrote. At this point, MSM was recording its own original material, although the group continued to play Latin and Top 40 favorites at live performances. The biggest hit from these early albums was a romantic Spanish ballad called "Renacer," which was popular with the audiences of the Spanish-language radio stations that played MSM's early records.

In 1980, Gloria's father died, after having been hospitalized for some time. But that same year, a joyous event occurred in the Estefans' lives: Their son, Nayib, was born. "Having a child gives you a sense of balance," Gloria discovered. "It makes you a lot more sensitive to other people. It keeps your feet on the ground." But the arrival of the baby did not change her commitment to her career, which by this point was firmly rooted in the music industry. Although she confirmed that Nayib was "more important to me than anything in the whole wide world," she added, "I don't feel that you're supposed to give up your career for your children. That's definitely a mistake. . . . Nine times out of ten, the children don't usually appreciate it when you do. And when you give up something of yourself, you're usually not as happy as you were before. And if you're not happy with yourself, it's very hard to make someone else happy."

For that reason, Estefan never stopped being a vital part of MSM. While Nayib was growing up during the 1980s, he spent many hours learning about the music business from the inside out; he listened to his mother try out new songs with her guitar, watched his parents and the rest of the band during performances, and sat in on studio sessions when songs were being recorded for albums.

Estefan drew on the close-knit structure of Latin family life to help her balance the responsibilities of motherhood and work. Her mother and sister were often available to help take care of Nayib, as were Emilio's aunts and cousins. Such family closeness has always been typical of the Estefans' professional life as well as

The Estefans' son, Nayib, was born in 1980, the same year that Gloria's father died. Though devoted to Nayib, Gloria decided not to let motherhood end her singing career. When she was on tour, she enlisted her mother, sister, and other family members to help out with child care.

their personal life, and a number of family members have worked for Emilio and Gloria. Becky Fajardo sometimes acts as her sister's personal assistant on the road during performance tours; José Estefan is Emilio's financial manager; Emilio's mother sometimes travels with the group to keep Gloria and Nayib company; and several cousins have worked in MSM's Miami offices.

Nayib's birth was not the only milestone for the Estefans in 1980. A short time after the baby was born, Emilio Estefan quit his job as director of Hispanic marketing at Bacardi Imports, where he had been earning $100,000 a year. Even with a new baby, he was willing to turn his back on security, a steady paycheck, and a corporate career because he felt that MSM held the potential for even greater success. He also believed that if the group was going to achieve that success, it needed his full-time attention. He and Gloria, along with Kiki Garcia and Juan Marcos Avila, formed the core of the group. Together they continued to create and perform music while Emilio worked tirelessly to promote them, looking for ways to turn their local fame into something bigger. In 1980, when he left Bacardi, Emilio took an important step in that direction by obtaining a recording contract with a major international company, CBS Records.

In order to understand the indirect path that Gloria Estefan followed to stardom during the 1980s, it is necessary to know something about the structure of the music business. Anyone who has ever listened to a radio realizes that each radio station has a different overall sound, determined by the station's choice of music. The type of music that a station generally plays is called its "format." Some stations have a classical format, whereas others specialize in jazz, country and western, or rock music. Within the broad category of rock music are many formats that are even more specialized: Typical examples are golden oldies, adult contemporary pop, easy listening, heavy metal, dance, black, and Top 40. The audience for each of these formats is called the "market." Areas with a significant Hispanic population have one or more radio stations with a Latin format, and record stores in those areas have Latin sections to serve the Hispanic market. This Latin market was the primary audience for MSM when the group began making records.

Most performers, and most songs, belong firmly to one particular format and appeal to one market. Recording industry publications, such as *Billboard* magazine, which ranks the popularity of albums and single songs each week, keep separate charts, or lists of the hits, for each format. Occasionally, however, a performer or group becomes popular in more than one market, and that performer's songs will be played on radio stations with different formats. One such performer is Michael Jackson, whose songs have been hits on both the black and pop charts. This phenomenon—the success of a performer in markets outside his or her primary audience—is called "crossover."

The recording industry is very fond of crossover artists, because they bring increased profits to the record companies. But company executives know that large-scale crossover successes are quite rare. For the most part, therefore, the record companies try to identify the market in which each performer is most likely to

Michael Jackson is a prime example of a "crossover" artist, one whose records defy categorization and achieve hit status on more than one chart—in Jackson's case, both the black music and pop music categories. Record company executives are in constant search of such performers, but they do not come along often.

succeed and then concentrate on making the performer a hit in that market. In the case of Latin music such as that played by the early Sound Machine, crossover was more than just rare—it was unheard of. Because of language and cultural barriers, no Latin group in the United States had ever achieved a big success with English-speaking listeners outside the Latin market. Gloria Estefan and MSM were eventually to change all that. But first they had to become international stars in the Latin market.

The division of CBS Records that signed MSM to a recording contract was Miami-based Discos CBS International, which was responsible for promoting Latin artists both in the United States and around the world. Although MSM had been performing and recording in both English and Spanish before they joined CBS, the record company decided to promote them internationally as a Spanish-speaking Latin band.

The decision was based on simple economics. There was a growing market for U.S.-style music throughout the Spanish–speaking countries of Central and South America. The record company executives felt that a group able to perform American disco and pop songs in Spanish would be a gold mine. "They thought we would sell better in Latin America if we sang in Spanish," Gloria Estefan explained. "But we kept the right to record in English because eventually we wanted to try again for the States. But first we decided to concentrate on the Latin American end because it was becoming very successful."

MSM did indeed become very successful in Latin America. In the years after signing with Discos CBS International, MSM spent a lot of time touring in Mexico, Puerto Rico, and Central and South America. At the same time, they performed in clubs and at concerts in Latin communities in the United States, particularly around their home base of Miami. But whereas at home they played to crowds of 3,000 and 4,000 people at a time, in other countries they filled soccer stadiums with crowds of 30,000 and 40,000. In fact, before very long they were one of the most popular acts throughout Latin America. They did especially well in Mexico, Peru, Venezuela, Argentina, Brazil, Honduras, and Panama. Their audiences were starved for U.S.-style popular music and loved hearing it in Spanish, whether it was original material composed by MSM or hit tunes from the United States translated for the Latin American audiences.

During this time, Gloria Estefan emerged as the band's unquestioned lead singer. For a long time, even before she and Emilio were married, she had been conquering her shyness and becoming more and more central to MSM. Her cousin Merci and Merci's husband, Raul Murciano, left the group in 1982; that same year, Gloria found herself in the forefront of the band, singing nearly all of its songs. It had taken a lot of time, patience, and effort, but Gloria Estefan would never again be found "playing maracas from the back," the way she had on her first appearance with the Miami Latin Boys.

MSM's success in Latin America gave Gloria and Emilio Estefan the opportunity to travel more widely than most people do at such an early age. They performed in almost every country in the Western Hemisphere during the early 1980s, and they had a number of memorable experiences. Gloria remembered most vividly something that happened in the Central American nation of Costa Rica. "We got an opportunity a long time ago to perform at a kind of boys' town that they have in Costa Rica. We had the benefit, and they took the money and built a new building for the boys' town and named it for us. When we went back two years later to do another concert, they made lunch for us and the kids sang for us and it was really nice. . . . It was a thrill to look back and see the guys [in the band] get all teary-eyed."

Gloria and MSM had a thrill of a different kind in 1985, when they were scheduled to appear before a crowd of 40,000 people at a stadium in El Salvador. That Central American country had been torn by violence and civil war for years, and being prepared for trouble was part of everyday life. When she went onstage, for

Gloria Estefan and the Miami Sound Machine (MSM) perform in Mexico City, Mexico. Although MSM enjoyed great success in Latin America, they were almost unknown in the United States before 1984: They performed and recorded in Spanish, and their producers at CBS Records considered them a purely Latin-oriented band.

example, Estefan was accompanied by three bodyguards carrying Uzi submachine guns. She and the other band members were understandably nervous about finding themselves in such a war-like environment. So when a series of explosions suddenly filled the sky above the stadium, Estefan and the other band members "hit the deck," as she put it. A moment later, they realized that the "explosions" were fireworks, which had been set off to welcome them to the stage. Sheepishly, they got to their feet and dusted themselves off while the crowd laughed and applauded.

Tours and live performances, however successful, are only half of the business of being a musical act. Singers and musicians must also release records; in fact, most of the tours and performances are scheduled to promote the records. Once they signed with CBS, MSM continued to make albums. Between 1981 and 1984, the group recorded four albums with Discos CBS International: *Renacer* (1981), *Otra Vez* (1981), *Río* (1982), and *A Toda Máquina* (1984). All of them were in Spanish. They contained mixtures of ballads, disco dance tunes, middle-of-the-road pop music, and more traditional Latin music, such as salsa and rumba numbers. The albums sold respectably in the Latin market in the United States and in Europe, and they did exceptionally well in Central and South America. In Peru, Panama, and a handful of other countries, MSM albums reached the number one position on the album-sales charts.

By 1984, MSM occupied an unusual position. They were one of the most popular and profitable acts in the world, but in their own country they were almost unknown outside the highly specialized Latin music market. Kiki Garcia and the Estefans were about to change that with a surprise hit song that paved the way for the music world's first Latin crossover success.

Gloria Estefan and the Miami Sound Machine broke into the pop market in 1984 with the single "Dr. Beat," recorded in English. The record was a smash hit and convinced Emilio Estefan that MSM could achieve a major following among English-speaking audiences.

CHAPTER SIX

Cutting Both Ways

In 1984, Kiki Garcia wrote a song called "Dr. Beat." It was a silly but likable song with a brisk, Latin-style dance beat and a repetitive, jingly chorus. Garcia wrote the words in English, and the band, as was their usual practice, translated them into Spanish. This time, however, they found that the lyrics simply would not translate into Spanish words that could be sung along with the music. Emilio Estefan thereupon decided that the Miami Sound Machine should release the song in English—perhaps it would draw Anglo listeners and be a big breakthrough for the band. He approached the record company with this plan in mind.

Discos CBS International was not pleased to think of its hit Spanish-language group making a record in English, but after many long discussions the company agreed to release "Dr. Beat" as the B side of a new MSM ballad in Spanish. (The B side of a single is the side that the producers think has the lesser chance of becoming a hit; the A side is the one that gets promoted.) The result surprised everyone. "Dr. Beat" sparked the interest of disc jockeys

Gloria Estefan, accompanied by Nayib and Emilio, is the first to leave her footprints on "Star Boulevard" in Scheveningen, the Netherlands. With the success of the Primitive Love *album in 1985, Gloria Estefan and the Miami Sound Machine were on their way to international stardom.*

at a bilingual radio station in Miami. While the station's Spanish disc jockeys were playing the ballad from the A side, the Anglo disc jockeys were playing "Dr. Beat." Soon, other pop stations in the area were giving the B side air time too. Then CBS released a 12-inch dance single of "Dr. Beat," which suddenly became a hit. The song reached the number 10 position on the dance music charts in the United States and turned into one of the most popular songs in Europe. It reached the Top Five in the pop market and number one in the dance market. For months it was the most-requested song in English discos, and it was so popular in Spain that MSM made a special trip there to promote it. (Ironically, because the record was in English, their Spanish hosts did not realize that the MSM members spoke Spanish, so the band was provided with translators.)

The success of "Dr. Beat" convinced Emilio Estefan that MSM could compete successfully in the English-language pop market. He decided that the group should release an album in English, and he pressed CBS Records to support this plan. With "Dr. Beat" bringing in money from all over, the record company agreed to back MSM's crossover venture. MSM was switched from Discos CBS International to Epic Records, the international rock music division of CBS. The band put together an album called *Eyes of Innocence*, with 10 songs, all in English, written by Garcia and the Estefans.

Eyes of Innocence was released in 1984. Although it contains some pleasant, danceable songs and one of Gloria Estefan's trademark lyrical ballads, the album was simply not good enough to make stars out of the Sound Machine. But their next album, *Primitive Love*, released in 1985, catapulted the band to stardom. To Anglo Americans who had never listened to Latin radio stations or records, it seemed as if MSM had just appeared out of nowhere with a string of hits from the album, one after the other. Only the band's loyal Hispanic following knew that MSM had been working toward that success for more than a decade.

The first smash hit from *Primitive Love* was a song called "Conga." It was the first MSM song that many Anglo listeners had heard; ironically, it was one of the most characteristically Latin songs the group had ever recorded. Conga songs are traditionally performed as the final dance numbers at Cuban parties or carnivals; everyone gets up and joins the dance at the end of the night. While MSM was touring in Europe to promote "Dr. Beat," they performed at a concert in the Netherlands, and they ended the show with some conga music. After the concert, on a plane bound from Amsterdam to London, Kiki Garcia thought about the audience's enthusiastic response to the conga sound. He started doodling with lyrics, and before long he had come up with "Come on, baby, shake your body, do the conga/I know you can't control yourself any longa!" This refrain was the beginning of MSM's breakthrough into the mainstream of American pop music.

At first, though, the recording industry had doubts about the song, because it did not fit neatly into an industry pigeonhole. Gloria remembers that when the group first performed it for one producer, he complained that it was too American for the Latin audiences and too Latin for the American audiences. "I said, 'Thank you, that's exactly what we are. We're a mix!'" she recalled.

As soon as *Primitive Love* was released, "Conga" started to climb the charts in the U.S. pop market. It peaked at the number 10 position, becoming the first MSM song to reach the Top 10 in the United States. The real milestone, however, came when "Conga" appeared on *Billboard* magazine's dance, pop, Latin, and black charts at the same time. It was the first single in recording history to do so—a crossover success indeed.

"Conga" introduced new rhythms to many listeners who were unfamiliar with Latin music. When Gloria Estefan and MSM went on tour to promote the album, audiences sometimes jumped to their feet and danced the conga to the band's closing number. For a while, according to Gloria, the unofficial record for the world's longest conga line was held by an audience in Burlington, Vermont, where more than 11,000 people did the conga while she sang. Later, that record was broken in spectacular fashion during a carnival in Miami: There, a crowd estimated at 119,000 danced the conga through the streets to the music of MSM.

"Conga" was a hit, but MSM was by no means established as a mainstream popular success. Hundreds of groups have burst onto the music scene with one big hit, only to vanish into obscurity a short while later. Some skeptics in the entertainment business thought that this might be the fate of MSM, which had succeeded with a novelty, an unusual dance number, but might be unable to follow it up. Gloria Estefan admitted that MSM had no intention of being categorized as "the conga band." She explained, "You can't build a career on congas, even in the Hispanic market. It's one thing, once a night, at the end, a catharsis for everybody, and that's it—you don't do ten."

A jubilant crowd at Miami's Calle Ocho Festival performs the conga, a traditional Cuban dance with African origins. MSM's "Conga" was the first single in recording history to appear on Billboard *magazine's dance, Latin, black, and pop charts at the same time.*

MSM demonstrated the broad range of their talents and proved the record industry skeptics wrong when the *Primitive Love* album produced two more Top 10 hits. One was "Bad Boy," a bouncy pop tune with a dance beat that reached the number eight position on the charts. The other was "Words Get in the Way," which reached number five. "Words" was the first of Gloria Estefan's English ballads to be played extensively to pop audiences, and it established her at once as a sensitive, skilled singer with a warm, graceful voice; her singing reminded many people of the late Karen Carpenter, a vocalist noted for romantic ballads. Music reviewer Bill Grein, writing in *Billboard*, claimed that "Words Get in the Way" was a crucial turning point for MSM because it proved that the group could produce "more than gimmicky, party-minded singles." "Words Get in the Way" was MSM's biggest hit in the United States up to that time, but it was special to Gloria Estefan for another reason as well. She wrote the song after she and

Emilio had had what she described as "an argument over some stupid thing," and she realized that "I hadn't said what I really meant to say. That's where I got the idea for 'Words Get in the Way.'" The song established Estefan's credentials as a songwriter and led the way for a series of ballads that would win her a song-writing award several years later. It also marked a transition in MSM's style. Beginning with "Words," the group shifted in the direction of simple, emotional ballads, although each album contained several rousing, Latin-influenced dance numbers and the fast-moving, lively pop songs that were staples of MSM concert appearances. Estefan admitted that although she loved singing and dancing to the up-tempo numbers, "ballads are basically what I'm about. I just feel you can express yourself more completely and eloquently in a ballad. It's easier to identify with someone else and form a bond with the audience."

Primitive Love sold 2 million copies. Following up on the album's success, Epic Records arranged a promotional tour for MSM that lasted through the spring, summer, and fall of 1986 and included 102 concerts in the United States, Central America, Europe, and Japan. While in Tokyo, the group represented the United States at the 15th annual Tokyo Music Fair, where their rendition of "Conga" won the first prize of $16,666. Estefan especially enjoyed performing in Japan. "In Japan they had told us, 'Don't feel bad if you just hear polite applause because the Japanese are very reserved people, that's just how they are,'" she recalled. "Then after the first song, they all jumped out of their seats and were dancing for the whole show. They even came up on the stage at the end of the show and danced with us. So I was pretty shocked."

The success of "Conga" and *Primitive Love* caused the Estefans to reflect on the meaning of the term *crossover*, which was used repeatedly in the media to describe the phenomenon of MSM's popularity. Sometimes, according to Gloria Estefan, people used the word negatively, as a form of belittlement. She pointed out that many critics accused MSM of doing "watered-down salsa" in order to appeal to the pop market. She objected to this characterization, saying that MSM had never claimed to be an authentic Cuban-style salsa band. She had always loved the music of salsa artists such as Tito Puente and Celia Cruz, but MSM had not tried to follow the strict salsa style. They drew on the music of Cruz, Puente, and others for inspiration, but they also had much in common with Spanish balladeer Julio Iglesias, who had achieved international success with mainstream sounds. The Estefans disliked the "crossover" label because it reinforced the impression that music must belong to one category or another. They preferred to think of their sound as a natural synthesis. "I don't feel Cuban or American," Gloria said. "I guess I feel Latin Miami." And Emilio often used a homely metaphor for the mixed sound he tried to achieve as a producer: He often described it as a blend of rice and beans (a traditional Cuban dish) and all-American hamburgers.

Demographic trends also probably played a part in the Miami Sound Machine's success. In the 1980s, Americans of Hispanic

Spanish balladeer Julio Iglesias, who appeals to both English-speaking and Latin audiences, was also a major influence on MSM. Although known principally for their uptempo dance tunes, MSM has also performed a number of ballads, many of them written by Gloria Estefan.

ancestry formed the fastest-growing minority group in the United States; during that decade, the number of Americans of Hispanic origin increased by 30 percent, to about 20 million. Experts predicted that in the year 2000, Hispanics would make up 15 percent of the total U.S. population. This growing cultural presence made Mexican, Puerto Rican, Cuban, and Central and South American influences more familiar in food, fashion, literature, and entertainment. On the music scene, Hispanic groups such as Los Lobos and Lisa Lisa and Cult Jam fused Latin sounds with traditional rock; Anglo musicians such as David Byrne and Paul Simon began using Brazilian instruments and rhythms. Anglo audiences seemed more receptive than ever before to Latin sounds, and some Hispanic entertainers, such as Rubén Blades, a Panamanian-born actor and musician noted for his Spanish albums, started recording in English in order to appeal to a broader range of listeners. The time was right for MSM.

Primitive Love brought a lot of changes into the Estefans' business and personal lives. For one thing, the album's success extended the group's fame far beyond Miami. The Pepsi-Cola company, which had helped sponsor the *Primitive Love* tour, paid MSM a seven-figure amount to make a Pepsi commercial to the tune of "Conga." MSM songs were featured in the soundtracks of two major movies: *Top Gun*, with Tom Cruise, and *Cobra*, with Sylvester Stallone. (The group's music was also used in the soundtracks of *Stakeout* and *Three Men and a Baby* a year or so later.) Miami was so proud of its new stars that the city council renamed the street where the Estefans lived Miami Sound Machine Boulevard.

Another change involved the band's production staff. Emilio Estefan's coproducers on *Primitive Love* were three Miamians named Joe Galdo, Rafael Vigil, and Lawrence Dermer, who called themselves "the Three Jerks." Galdo and Dermer had appeared as guest musicians on *Eyes of Innocence*. After that, the Three Jerks were working on a soundtrack for an exercise album with a salsa beat. Estefan heard their work and hired them to help him produce *Primitive Love*, some of the songs on the MSM album, including the hit "Bad Boy," were versions of the Jerks' "salsa-cize" tunes. Later on, the Three Jerks claimed credit for developing what came to be called "the Miami sound," a blend of disco and Latin influences with many layers of synthesizer music added to each track in the studio.

The huge popular success of *Primitive Love* also motivated Gloria Estefan to work even harder on her image and appearance. She had lost quite a bit of weight over the years, so much that when she went to the 10-year reunion of her high school class, many of her former classmates did not recognize her. But in the late 1980s, with fitness established as the new American ideal and entertainers working out like professional athletes, she felt she should lose still more weight and cultivate a more athletic look. With the help of a personal trainer, who got her running and coached her through daily workouts, Estefan got her weight down to 102 pounds and kept it there. She watched her diet carefully and worked out every day on an exercise bicycle, bringing it with her whenever she traveled or went on tour.

Estefan was encouraged in this effort by her promoters at the record company, who knew that she would have to make videos to compete with those of Madonna and Janet Jackson if she were to succeed in the teenage market. A manager at Epic Records named Larry Stessel was assigned to help develop a strong image for the group. Stessel explained the importance of image this way: "You can make the best car in the world, [one] that gets 75 miles to the gallon and never breaks down, but if it looks terrible it'll never sell. The same is true for a recording artist." Stessel talked to the Estefans about the need for the group to have a sharper focus, a personality for the public to recognize. From that time on the band was referred to as Gloria Estefan and the Miami Sound Machine— with the emphasis on Gloria Estefan.

Epic Records was pleased with the success of *Primitive Love* and hoped to follow it with an even more successful album. Their hopes

were realized in 1987, two years after *Primitive Love*, when Gloria
Estefan and MSM released the album *Let It Loose*. It sold 3 million
copies and produced four Top 10 hits: "1-2-3" and "Rhythm Is
Gonna Get You," which are upbeat dance songs ("Rhythm" is based
on a Latin beat called *bembe*), and "Anything for You" and "Can't
Stay Away from You," which are wistful, lovelorn ballads. A fifth
song, "Betcha Say That," another lively pop number, made it into
the Top 40.

Just as "Words Get in the Way" had been a landmark on *Primitive Love*, "Anything for You" was a special achievement on *Let It
Loose*, a triumph for both of the Estefans. Gloria wrote it hastily,
almost casually, in a hamburger joint before she was scheduled to
begin work at the recording studio. She recorded the vocals of the
song in one take, and Emilio and the other producers stayed up all
night to perfect the musical accompaniment. Epic Records did not
want to include the song on the album, feeling that it was too
simple and spare. Emilio Estefan disagreed. He believed in the
song and thought it could be a hit. He insisted that it be included,
and Gloria, trusting both in her song and in her husband's business sense, backed him up. Reluctantly, Epic agreed to let the
Estefans do it their way, and "Anything for You" went on to become
the group's first number one hit. "When I think how hard I worked
on other songs, like 'Can't Stay Away From You,' it's really amazing," Gloria Estefan told a reporter. "I can't believe it's number 1 in
the country."

Let It Loose stayed on the charts for more than two years in the
United States. It was also a hit around the world. In England, where
"Anything for You" was on the charts for a year, *Let It Loose* was
withdrawn from stores and repackaged under the title *Anything for
You*, upon which it sold out almost overnight. It also did well in the
Netherlands, Scandinavia, and Japan. Gloria Estefan spent a total
of 20 months on tour to promote the album, performing in the
United States, Canada, Japan, and Southeast Asia.

One highlight of the tour, in May 1988, was an appearance in
the Demilitarized Zone between North Korea and South Korea.

"Three of our band, and Bob Hope and Brooke Shields, were flown there to give a special concert for about 2,000 American soldiers," Estefan remembered. The show was a success—except that the performance was being filmed for showing at the Olympics in Seoul, South Korea, and the cameraman had a little trouble fitting Shields, who is nearly six feet tall, and Estefan, who is barely more than five feet tall, into the same shot. MSM's world tour ended with two huge concerts in Miami. Gloria Estefan's hometown fans turned out by the thousands to welcome her back. Those concerts were filmed for presentation on the Showtime cable television network and later released as the *Homecoming Concert* video.

Estefan jokes around during the filming of a music video in 1989. During her first video in 1987, she had to perform in a romantic scene with a handsome young actor. Estefan found the experience embarrassing but forced herself to see it through: "I told myself I was on the line, I had to do this. And do it right."

The *Let It Loose* tour marked a significant change for Gloria Estefan. For the first time since her marriage, she was not accompanied by Emilio. After the recording of *Let It Loose*, Emilio Estefan had decided to withdraw from his role as one of the group's percussionists so that he could concentrate on production. In addition to producing all of MSM's records, his production company has also made records for Clarence Clemons of Bruce Springsteen's E Street Band, Julio Iglesias, Japanese jazz guitarist Takanaka, and Japanese pop singer Seiko, among others. Because he was no longer performing, Emilio was able to stay home in Miami with Nayib, who did not want to leave his school and his Little League team during the tour. Gloria agreed that it would be much better for Nayib to be home with one parent than to be on the road with both parents. She channeled her occasional feelings of loss and loneliness into songwriting, preparing a handful of aching-heart ballads for the next album.

The conclusion of the *Let It Loose* tour brought changes in the personnel of MSM. Kiki Garcia, the last remaining member of the core combo other than Gloria Estefan, left MSM, complaining that the group had turned into a massive business enterprise and star vehicle. "There is no Miami Sound Machine," Garcia contended.

Clarence Clemons (center) performing with Bruce Springsteen and the E Street Band in 1986. In 1988, Emilio Estefan branched out to produce records for Clemons and a number of other artists. In order to concentrate on this work, he stopped performing with MSM.

"There is Gloria and Emilio telling a bunch of hired musicians what to do."

Around the same time Garcia was leaving MSM, Emilio Estefan and the Three Jerks were nominated for the American Music Award as Best Producers of 1988. The award went to Whitney Houston's producer, but the nomination was a great honor. Gloria and MSM did better: They took home the award for Best Pop/Rock Group of the year. After the awards ceremony, Emilio Estefan offered the Three Jerks a contract to work exclusively with him and MSM. When they refused because they wanted to pursue other projects while producing MSM's next album, Estefan abruptly ended their connection with the group. His former coproducers responded bitterly to their dismissal, claiming that Estefan had taken too much of the credit for creating a hit sound that was really their work.

Estefan immediately set to work on a new album with different coproducers—Jorge Casas and Clay Ostwald, two musicians who had been part of the ensemble on *Let It Loose.* In one of the three recording studios in MSM's new office complex in Miami, they produced a 1989 album called *Cuts Both Ways.* Seven of the 10 songs on the album were written by Gloria Estefan. "Miami Sound Machine" did not appear on the front cover of the album, and most music stores filed the records, tapes, and compact discs under *E*, not *M*.

Cuts Both Ways took its name from one of the songs on the album, yet it was also a pun. In record industry jargon, a "cut" is one song on an album, and this album contained cuts, or songs, in both English and Spanish, although most of them were in English. Gloria Estefan also made several Spanish videos of songs on the album that have appeared both in the United States and in Latin America. Putting her gift for languages to good use, she even recorded several songs in Portuguese for release in Brazil, where Portuguese is spoken. Her writing for the album earned the 1989 Songwriter of the Year Award from BMI, an organization that sells

Estefan rehearses with Spanish opera star Plácido Domingo before a 1988 concert in New York's Central Park. By 1988, Estefan had unquestionably become the focus of the Miami Sound Machine. Kiki Garcia, who left the band at this time, complained that MSM had become too much of a star vehicle.

performance rights to popular music and deals with nearly all performers and composers in the field. "I think the award will help people look at me in a different way," she said. "A lot of times, folks just listen to the music and don't pay any attention to the lyrics. It's nice being honored this way, because it sort of makes people stand up and take notice."

Epic Records had high hopes for *Cuts Both Ways*, expecting the album to stay on the charts for several years and to earn $5 million or $6 million. Both Epic and the Estefans were thrilled when a single from the album, a ballad called "Don't Wanna Lose You," reached number one on the charts, the second of the group's songs to do so. Another song from *Cuts Both Ways*, "Get on Your Feet," a rousing, up-tempo number sung by the whole band, also reached the Top 10. The tour that the Estefans and Epic Records had planned to promote *Cuts Both Ways* took its name from this song.

The tour began in Europe and got off to a good start. In September and October 1989, Gloria Estefan performed at a string of sold-out concerts in England, Scotland, the Netherlands, and Belgium. This leg of the tour concluded with three nights at

Wembley Stadium in London. This time, Nayib wanted to come along on the tour, so the Estefans traveled as a family.

Problems set in when the U.S. leg of the tour got under way in the late fall. Gloria was suffering from influenza and a sore throat, but she was reluctant to cancel any concert dates, so she went ahead with the schedule. She got sicker and sicker, however, and she had to cancel two appearances in the Midwest because she could not sing. At that point she consulted a throat specialist, who gave her some very serious news: The constant coughing caused by her sore throat had ruptured a blood vessel in her throat, and an infection had set in. The doctor told her that in order to avoid permanent damage to her throat she would have to stop singing for at least two months and should not even talk for two weeks. The tour was postponed, and Estefan returned to Miami to get over her infection and regain her strength.

She was back in action early in January 1990, appearing as one of the hosts of the American Music Awards show. A few weeks later, she performed at another music industry special event, the Grammy Awards. On the strength of "Don't Wanna Lose You," Gloria Estefan was nominated for the Grammy Award for Best Female Vocal Performance, and Emilio Estefan was nominated for the Grammy Award for Producer of the Year. Although neither won, the nominations added a spark to their renewed American concert tour. Early in March, at New York City's fashionable "21" Club, CBS Records honored Gloria Estefan and MSM with the Crystal Globe Award, which the company gives to artists who sell 5 million or more records outside their home country. The award had been presented only 27 times since its inception in 1974.

For the next several weeks, Gloria Estefan was constantly on the move as she finished up the U.S. tour, taking time out only for a visit to the White House, where she was praised for her antidrug work by President George Bush. She was very much looking forward to a short break before beginning a tour of South America to promote *Cuts Both Ways*. But the accident on a snowy Pennsylvania road on March 20 changed everything.

Gloria Estefan is greeted by her son, Nayib, at Miami International Airport on April 4, 1990, after she was discharged from the Hospital for Joint Diseases in New York. In the following weeks, Estefan slowly regained her strength and mobility under the guidance of a physical therapist.

CHAPTER SEVEN

Back on Her Feet

As she lay in a hospital room in Scranton, listening to the doctors tell her that her back was broken, Gloria Estefan remembered what had flashed through her mind in the seconds after the impact: "Here it is. This is the thing I've been waiting for.

"All my life I've been afraid of becoming an invalid," explained Estefan. She had never forgotten what it was like nursing her father through his long, slow decline. "He was a very athletic, strong, and handsome man," she remembered. "For years and years I watched him weaken and die. I saw what it did to the people around him—to his family. I've had a premonition all my life that I would become a burden to the people I love."

When the doctors told Emilio Estefan that his wife's back was broken, he fainted. A few moments later, when he had regained consciousness, he was wheeled, white-faced and distraught, into Gloria's room. His hand was bandaged where he had suffered a cut in the crash, but he was so concerned about Gloria and Nayib that he neglected to have a complete physical examination himself. It was not until almost a week later that the doctors discovered he had suffered a separated shoulder and a broken rib.

For the moment, his attention and Gloria's were riveted on the doctors, who were explaining several ways of treating her injury. Two of the vertebrae in the middle of her spine were fractured. According to Dr. Harry Schmaltz, who treated her at the Scranton Community Medical Center, the accident came very close to severing Estefan's spinal cord. "Another half inch of movement of the spine," he reported, "and she'd be completely paralyzed." The standard form of treatment for that type of injury would have required that Estefan be immobilized in a body cast for six months while her bones knit. This method offered little hope of a full recovery. A newer kind of treatment, however, presented greater risks but also greater potential for recovery. This treatment involved surgery to the spine. Surgery posed the danger of infection and, possibly, permanent paralysis. On the other hand, an operation would allow the doctors to determine just how badly Estefan's spinal nerves had been damaged and perhaps allow them to repair the two broken vertebrae. Gloria decided to have the surgery.

The next question involved the choice of surgeon and hospital. "It was a difficult decision," Estefan remembered. "I didn't want the doctors in Scranton to feel I didn't trust them, but I wanted a surgeon who did this operation daily." After several hours of feverish telephoning to friends, contacts, and orthopedic surgeons (who specialize in bone surgery) all over the country, Emilio came up with the name of Dr. Michael Neuwirth at New York City's Hospital for Joint Diseases. Neuwirth flew to Scranton at once to examine Estefan and accompanied her as she was transferred to New York by helicopter the following day. Neuwirth marveled at Estefan's strength and good nature. "The way she tolerates the pain!" he told an audience of more than 50 reporters and newscasters at a press conference in the hospital. "Riding in a helicopter with a broken back for 45 minutes must have been uncomfortable. There was not a peep of complaint."

In fact, Estefan was in constant pain. Almost as soon as she arrived at the Scranton Community Medical Center, she had been hooked up to life-support machines, because the organs of her body had simply shut down in the face of the massive trauma to her spine. She was given drugs to kill the pain, but they did not kill all of it, and they never lasted long enough. "I began a horrible cycle of pain and painkillers," she recalled. But she added that the pain was offset by the flood of get-well wishes that began to arrive as soon as the account of the accident was made public.

The news brought shock and sorrow to Miami. Radio stations began playing Estefan's songs nonstop; the *Miami Herald* printed a full-page get-well message for her fans to cut out and send to her; and a television station established a 900 telephone number for get-well calls. But reaction to the accident was not confined to Estefan's hometown. She received more than 48,000 cards, faxes, and letters from all over the world, in addition to 3,000 telegrams and 4,000 floral arrangements. Fellow musicians Elton John, Madonna, Bruce Springsteen, Eric Clapton, Diana Ross, Cyndi Lauper, Whitney Houston, and Celia Cruz telephoned or visited the hospital. President Bush called twice and prayed with Gloria over the phone.

The majority of the messages that were sent to Estefan, however, came from everyday fans and well-wishers. A typical example was a fax that read, "If you can get out of Cuba, betcha can get out of this one": It was signed, "Two Cubans and a bunch of guys from the United Nations." Estefan said that this outpouring of concern touched her deeply and made her ordeal much more bearable: "It was like an energy I could feel in the hospital. It helped me bear all that pain." Her room was overrun with flowers, so Estefan kept some white roses for herself and shared the rest with other patients in the hospital and with the AIDS ward of the local Veterans Administration hospital.

Dr. Neuwirth performed the surgery on March 23. The operation took nearly four hours. First, Neuwirth made a 14-inch in-

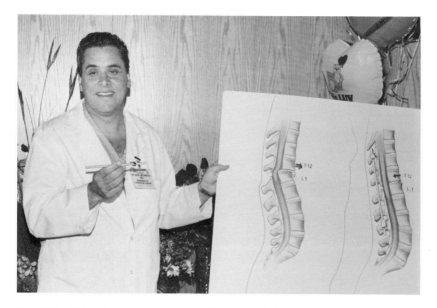

Dr. Michael Neuwirth shows reporters a diagram explaining the injury to Estefan's spine. In his right hand, Neuwirth holds one of the steel rods that he was to insert during the following day's operation; with the rods stabilizing her spinal column, Estefan's broken vertebrae would be able to heal.

cision down the middle of Estefan's back. Then, using a technique that had come into use in the early 1980s, Neuwirth inserted two eight-inch stainless steel rods, one on either side of the spine, to support the broken vertebrae and relieve the pressure on Estefan's spinal nerves. These rods will remain in place permanently; Estefan later joked that her husband started calling her RoboCop because of her metal parts and that she was resigned to setting off metal detectors in airports for the rest of her life.

Neuwirth next removed some bone tissue from Estefan's pelvic bone (through the same incision), ground it up, and inserted it next to the rods, where it will eventually fuse together with the bits of broken vertebrae to form a stiff band of bone. Finally, a plastic surgeon closed the incision with more than 400 stitches. Almost at once, Neuwirth could tell that the operation had been successful. Before the surgery, electronic monitors had shown that the injury to Estefan's spine was interfering with the function of nerves in her legs and on her left side; this neurological function began to improve immediately after the rods were in place. By that evening, Neuwirth was able to announce that if Estefan's recovery went as well as the operation, she could expect to regain 95 to 100 percent of her former mobility.

On April 4, 1990, Gloria Estefan returned to Miami and devoted herself to recovery with the same intensity she had earlier brought to performing. Under the guidance of her doctors, she worked with a physical therapist and used stretching and aerobic exercises in her swimming pool to gain strength without placing stress on her spine. She took pleasure in each new achievement—the ability to bend over the sink to wash her face, for example, or to put her shoes on by herself.

Estefan expected to be able to perform in early 1991. She planned a major concert tour to celebrate her recovery and to give a boost to the sales of *Cuts Both Ways*. Even before the accident, she had written several songs for a forthcoming album, and during her recovery she continued to write and to experiment with music on the piano and a computerized synthesizer. On a personal level, the Estefans had been planning to have another child but realized that they would have to wait a year or more for Gloria's back to be fully healed.

While planning her return to the concert stage, Estefan contemplated another kind of crossover—this time into film. This path had been taken by such pop singers as Barbra Streisand, Madonna, Diana Ross, Neil Diamond, and Sting, all of whom had embarked on acting careers while continuing to make records. With music videos blurring the distinction between the music and film worlds, more and more singers are doubling as actors. Thomas Mottola, president of CBS Records, stated that Estefan could certainly branch out into film acting and perhaps even do a Broadway show. And Jorge Pinos of the William Morris Agency revealed that a number of screenwriters and producers had sent in scripts they thought suitable for Estefan; although Estefan had not asked to look at any of the scripts, Pinos suggested that she might eventually appear in a musical film.

Clearly, Estefan was determined that the accident would not have any long-term effect on her life or her work. "I don't plan on changing my stage routine," she insisted. "I will still, I hope, be able to dance and move spontaneously, as the music inspires me." One change would certainly be made, however: She vowed that any vehicle she rode in would be equipped with restraints and seat belts. For months after the accident, she was nervous whenever she rode in a car. "I can't stop looking out the rearview mirror,"

By September 1990, Estefan was well enough to make public appearances and was planning a concert tour for 1991. "When I think of what could have happened," she said, "I feel better—and luckier—every day."

she admitted. "I keep thinking that when we were hit we were so very vulnerable." The Estefans have filed a million-dollar lawsuit against Canadian resident Gerardo Samuels, the driver of the truck that rammed into the Odyssey. According to the Pennsylvania State Police, Samuels's truck had faulty brakes and was being driven at an unsafe speed.

In September 1990, Gloria Estefan made her first public appearance since the accident. In a film clip that was taped in Miami, she greeted viewers of Jerry Lewis's Labor Day Telethon for the Muscular Dystrophy Association. In an interview, she reflected on the events that had almost ended her career and her life. "Ironically, I'm more relaxed now," she said. "I was always thinking things were going too well. Something was going to happen—and now it has. I figure I'm good for another few years. And after such pain, I'm enjoying every second; every little thing is just that much more fun. When I think of what could have happened, I feel better—and luckier—every day." At every opportunity during her recovery, Gloria Estefan promised her fans that she would soon return to the studio and the concert stage in better shape than ever before. "It'll take a lot of hard work," she said, "but I've never been afraid of hard work." Her life and career have provided ample evidence of that.

Discography

Hit Singles (with highest chart position)

"Conga"	*Primitive Love*	10
"Bad Boy"	*Primitive Love*	8
"Words Get in the Way"	*Primitive Love*	5
"Falling in Love (Uh-Oh)"	*Primitive Love*	25
"1-2-3"	*Let It Loose*	3
"Anything for You"	*Let It Loose*	1
"Can't Stay Away from You"	*Let It Loose*	6
"Betcha Say That"	*Let It Loose*	36
"Rhythm Is Gonna Get You"	*Let It Loose*	5
"Don't Wanna Lose You"	*Cuts Both Ways*	1
"Get on Your Feet"	*Cuts Both Ways*	10

Chronology

September 1, 1957   Gloria Fajardo is born in Havana, Cuba

1959   Communist revolutionary Fidel Castro takes control of Cuba; the Fajardo family leaves for the United States

April 1961   José Fajardo, Gloria's father, is captured in Cuba during the Bay of Pigs invasion

December 1962   Fajardo and other prisoners return to the United States from prison in Cuba

1966   Emilio Estefan leaves Cuba for Spain at age 13; he arrives in the United States in 1967

1974   Emilio forms a musical group called the Miami Latin Boys

1975   Gloria Fajardo meets Emilio and begins singing with his band

1976   The band is renamed Miami Sound Machine (MSM)

1978   Miami Sound Machine releases its first album; Gloria graduates from the University of Miami; Gloria and Emilio are married

1980   Nayib Estefan is born

1981–83	MSM records four albums in Spanish for Discos CBS International
1984	MSM releases its first English-language album, *Eyes of Innocence*; "Dr. Beat" becomes a hit
1985	*Primitive Love* album, featuring "Conga," is released by MSM
1986	Representing the United States at the 15th annual Tokyo Music Festival, MSM wins the grand prize with "Conga"; MSM wins American Music Awards in the Best New Pop Artists and Top Pop Singles Artists categories
1987	*Let It Loose* album is released
1988	Gloria wins BMI Songwriter of the Year award; she and MSM win the American Music Award for Best Pop/Rock Group of the year; Emilio Estefan is nominated for an American Music Award for Best Producer of the Year; *Billboard* magazine calls MSM the second most popular group in the United States
1989	*Cuts Both Ways* album is released
January 1990	Gloria hosts the American Music Awards broadcast
March 1990	Gloria's back is broken in a highway accident; after surgery, a full recovery is predicted
September 1990	Gloria appears on the Jerry Lewis Muscular Dystrophy Association telethon, her first public appearance since the accident; plans a new album and a tour in 1991

Further Reading

Adrianson, Doug. "Race to the Top of the Charts." *Miami Herald*, May 7, 1988.

Aros, Andrew. *The Latin Music Handbook*. Diamond Bar, CA: Applause Publications, 1978.

Chase, Gilbert. *Guide to the Music of Latin America*. New York: AMS Press, 1962.

Coto, Juan Carlos. "1-2-3 with Gloria." *Miami Herald*, September 30, 1988.

Dougherty, Steve, et al. "Gloria Estefan's Amazing Recovery." *People*, June 25, 1990.

Estefan, Gloria, and Kathryn Casey. "My Miracle." *Ladies Home Journal*, August 1990.

Grenet, Emilio. *Popular Cuban Music*. New York: Gordon Press, 1986.

Harrington, Richard. "Miami Voice." *Washington Post*, July 17, 1988.

Lacayo, Richard. "A Surging New Spirit." *Time*, July 11, 1988.

McLane, Daissan. "The Power and the Gloria." *Rolling Stone*, June 14, 1990.

Marx, Linda. "Throw the Switch on the Miami Sound Machine and Pop Go the Hit Singles." *People*, October 27, 1986.

Milward, John. "Gloria Estefan: Living in Two Worlds." *TV Guide*, January 20, 1990.

Nash, Jesse. "For Gloria Estefan, Family, Friends, and Work Are 1-2-3 in Order of Importance." *New York Tribune*, September 14, 1988.

Roberts, John S. *The Latin Tinge: The Impact of Latin-American Music on the United States*. New York: Oxford University Press, 1979.

Index

REBECCA STEFOFF is a Philadelphia-based freelance writer and editor who has published more than 40 nonfiction books for young adults. She has also served as the editorial director of Chelsea House's PLACES AND PEOPLES OF THE WORLD and LET'S DISCOVER CANADA series. Stefoff received her M.A. and Ph.D. degrees in English from the University of Pennsylvania, where she taught for three years.

RODOLFO CARDONA is professor of Spanish and comparative literature at Boston University. A renowned scholar, he has written many works of criticism, including *Ramón, a Study of Gómez de la Serna and His Works* and *Visión del esperpento: Teoría y practica del esperpento en Valle-Inclán.* Born in San José, Costa Rica, he earned his B.A. and M.A. from Louisiana State University and received a Ph.D. from the University of Washington. He has taught at Case Western Reserve University, the University of Pittsburgh, the University of Texas at Austin, the University of New Mexico, and Harvard University.

JAMES COCKCROFT is currently a visiting professor of Latin American and Caribbean studies at the State University of New York at Albany. A three-time Fulbright scholar, he earned a Ph.D. from Stanford University and has taught at the University of Massachusetts, the University of Vermont, and the University of Connecticut. He is the author or coauthor of numerous books on Latin American subjects, including *Neighbors in Turmoil: Latin America, The Hispanic Experience in the United States: Contemporary Issues and Perspectives,* and *Outlaws in the Promised Land: Mexican Immigrant Workers and America's Future.*

PICTURE CREDITS